PRIMARY MATHEMATICS 2B
TEXTBOOK

W9-AHF-552

Primary Mathematics Project Team

Project Director
Dr Kho Tek Hong

Team Members
Chee Kum Hoong, Hector
Liang Hin Hoon
Lim Eng Tann
Lim Hui Cheng, Rosalind
Ng Hwee Wan
Ng Siew Lee
Thong Chee Hing

Curriculum Planning & Development Division
Ministry of Education, Singapore

FEDERAL PUBLICATIONS

Original edition published under the title Primary Mathematics 2B
© 1982 Curriculum Planning & Development Division
Ministry of Education, Singapore
Published by Times Media Private Limited
This American Edition
© 2003 Times Media Private Limited

Times Media Private Limited
A member of Times Publishing Limited
Times Centre, 1 New Industrial Road, Singapore 536196
Customer Service Hotline: (65) 6213 9106
E-mail: fps@tpl.com.sg
Website: www.timesone.com.sg/fpl

Distributed by
SingaporeMath.com Inc
404 Beavercreek Road #225
Oregon City, OR 97045
U.S.A.
Website: http://www.singaporemath.com

First published 2003
Second impression 2003
Reprinted 2004

ISBN 981-01-8499-9

Illustrated by: Myo Myint

Printed in Singapore by Times Graphics Pte Ltd

ACKNOWLEDGEMENTS

The project team would like to record their thanks to the following:

- members of the Primary Mathematics Team who developed the first edition and second edition of the package
- members of the Steering Committee for the second edition of the package
- teachers who tested the materials in the package and provided useful insights and suggestions
- Educational Technology Division, for the design and production of the audio-visual components of the package
- all those who have helped in one way or another in the development and production of the package

Our special thanks to Richard Askey, Professor of Mathematics (University of Wisconsin, Madison), Yoram Sagher, Professor of Mathematics (University of Illinois, Chicago), and Madge Goldman, President (Gabriella and Paul Rosenbaum Foundation), for their indispensable advice and suggestions in the production of Primary Mathematics (U.S. Edition).

PREFACE

Primary Mathematics (U.S. Edition) comprises textbooks and workbooks. The main feature of this package is the use of the **Concrete ➡ Pictorial ➡ Abstract** approach. The students are provided with the necessary learning experiences beginning with the concrete and pictorial stages, followed by the abstract stage to enable them to learn mathematics meaningfully. This package encourages active thinking processes, communication of mathematical ideas and problem solving.

This textbook is accompanied by a workbook. It comprises 9 units. Each unit is divided into parts: **❶**, **❷**, . . . Each part starts with a meaningful situation for communication and is followed by specific learning tasks numbered 1, 2, . . . The sign Workbook Exercise is used to link the textbook to the workbook exercises.

Practice exercises are designed to provide the students with further practice after they have done the relevant workbook exercises. Review exercises are provided for cumulative reviews of concepts and skills. All the practice exercises and review exercises are optional exercises.

The color patch ■ is used to invite active participation from the students and to faciliate oral discussion. The students are advised not to write on the color patches.

CONTENTS

Addition and Subtraction

1 Finding the Missing Number

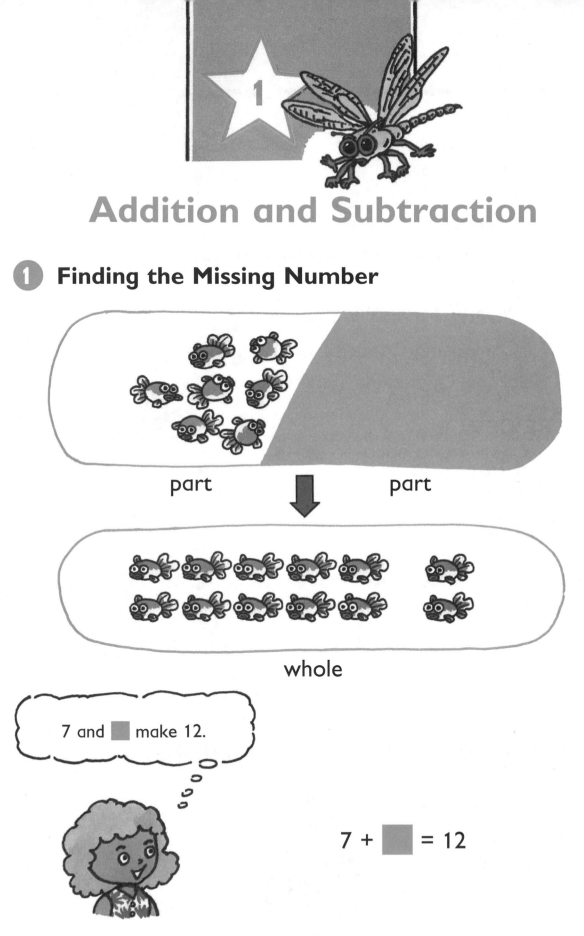

part   part

whole

7 and ■ make 12.

$7 + ■ = 12$

To find one part, we subtract.

$12 - 7 = 5$

1.

How many flowers do I take away?

$20 - \boxed{} = 12$

2. Complete the number sentences.

(a)

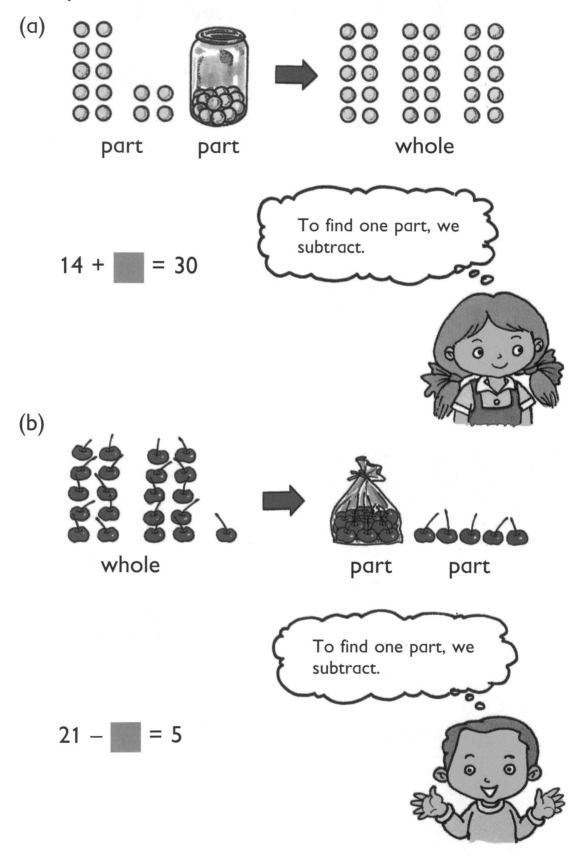

part   part   whole

14 + ▢ = 30

To find one part, we subtract.

(b)

whole   part   part

21 − ▢ = 5

To find one part, we subtract.

8

(c)

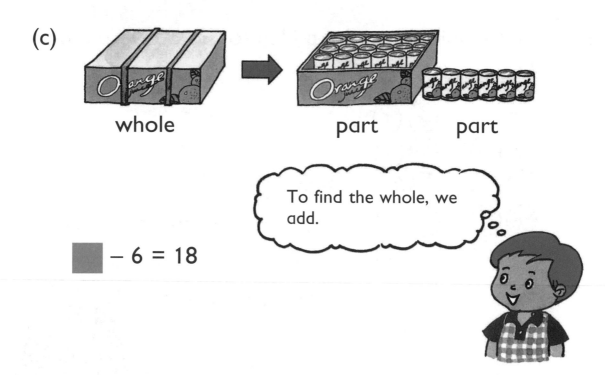

whole   part   part

To find the whole, we add.

$\blacksquare - 6 = 18$

3. Find the missing number in each of the following:

(a) $4 + \blacksquare = 13$ (b) $20 - \blacksquare = 13$

(c) $9 + \blacksquare = 39$ (d) $47 - \blacksquare = 19$

(e) $\blacksquare + 8 = 15$ (f) $\blacksquare - 7 = 10$

(g) $\blacksquare + 14 = 60$ (h) $\blacksquare - 16 = 40$

Workbook Exercise 1

4. There are **68** saga seeds in a bottle.
   How many more saga seeds are needed to make 100?

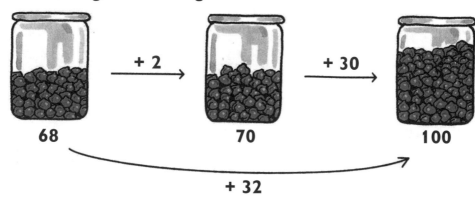

5. What number must be added to 53 to give the answer 100?

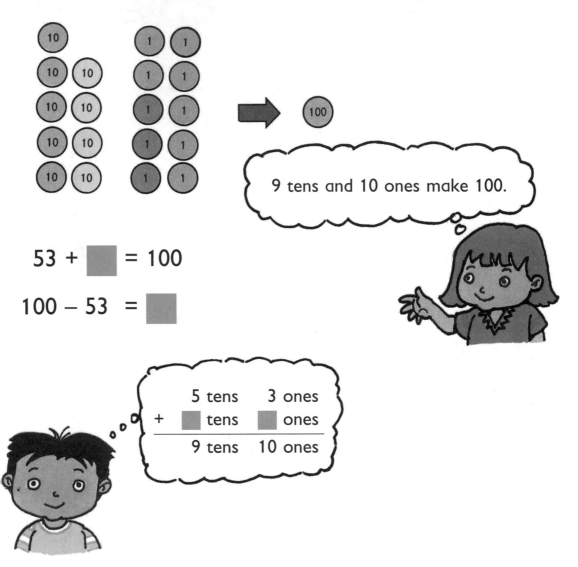

9 tens and 10 ones make 100.

$53 + \boxed{} = 100$

$100 - 53 = \boxed{}$

	5 tens	3 ones
+	$\boxed{}$ tens	$\boxed{}$ ones
	9 tens	10 ones

6. Find the missing number in each of the following:

(a) $34 + \boxed{} = 100$

(b) $76 + \boxed{} = 100$

(c) $\boxed{} + 82 = 100$

(d) $\boxed{} + 9 = 100$

7. Find the value of

(a) $100 - 26$ (b) $100 - 61$ (c) $100 - 42$
(d) $100 - 96$ (e) $100 - 2$ (f) $100 - 8$

Workbook Exercise 2

PRACTICE 1A

1. Find the missing number in each of the following:

   (a) ▢ + 25 = 40   (b) 23 − ▢ = 6

   (c) ▢ + 17 = 56   (d) 43 − ▢ = 21

   (e) 58 + ▢ = 72   (f) ▢ − 79 = 11

   (g) 46 + ▢ = 100   (h) ▢ − 18 = 54

   (i) ▢ + 25 = 100   (j) 100 − ▢ = 93

   (k) 63 + ▢ = 100   (l) 100 − ▢ = 57

2. Find the value of each of the following:

   (a) 100 − 38   (b) 100 − 99   (c) 100 − 98
   (d) 100 − 4   (e) 100 − 9   (f) 100 − 3

3. A farmer had 215 ducks.
   After selling some of them, he had 36 ducks left.
   How many ducks did he sell?

4. Mr. Brown bought a fan for $127.
   He had $53 left.
   How much money did he have at first?

5. A cabbage weighs 324 g.
   A cucumber weighs 86 g less than the cabbage.
   (a) What is the weight of the cucumber?
   (b) Find the total weight of the cabbage and the
       cucumber.

2 Methods for Mental Addition

What number is 20 more than 356?

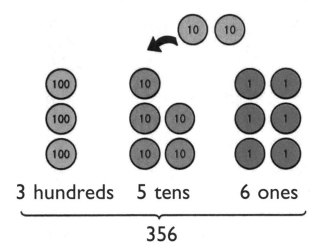

3 hundreds　　5 tens　　6 ones

356

Add 2 tens to 356.

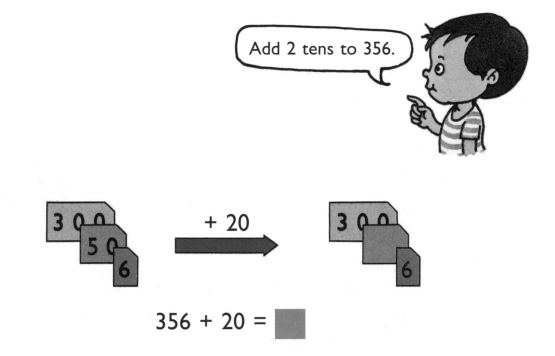

356 + 20 =

What number is 2 more than 356?

What number is 200 more than 356?

1. Find the value of

   (a) 43 + 6   (b) 38 + 7   (c) 56 + 5
   (d) 20 + 30   (e) 40 + 50   (f) 80 + 60
   (g) 24 + 30   (h) 43 + 50   (i) 87 + 60

   Workbook Exercise 3

2. Find the value of

   (a) 153 + 9   (b) 278 + 5   (c) 605 + 7
   (d) 320 + 60   (e) 235 + 70   (f) 164 + 50
   (g) 200 + 200 (h) 500 + 300 (i) 400 + 500
   (j) 256 + 200 (k) 504 + 300 (l) 465 + 500

   Workbook Exercise 4

3. Add 43 and 26.

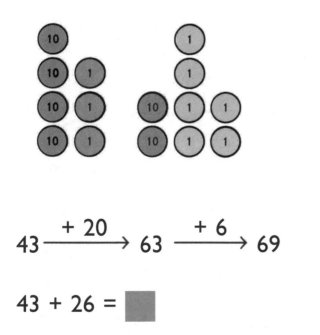

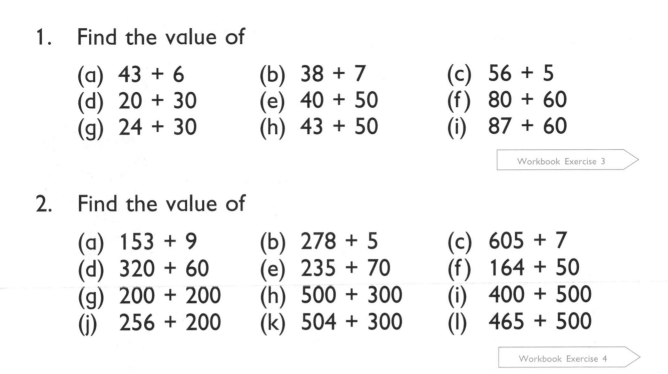

   43 $\xrightarrow{\ +\ 20\ }$ 63 $\xrightarrow{\ +\ 6\ }$ 69

   43 + 26 = ▢

4. Find the value of

   (a) 51 + 18   (b) 65 + 12   (c) 72 + 16
   (d) 32 + 47   (e) 56 + 23   (f) 24 + 35

Workbook Exercise 5

5. Add 99 and 4.

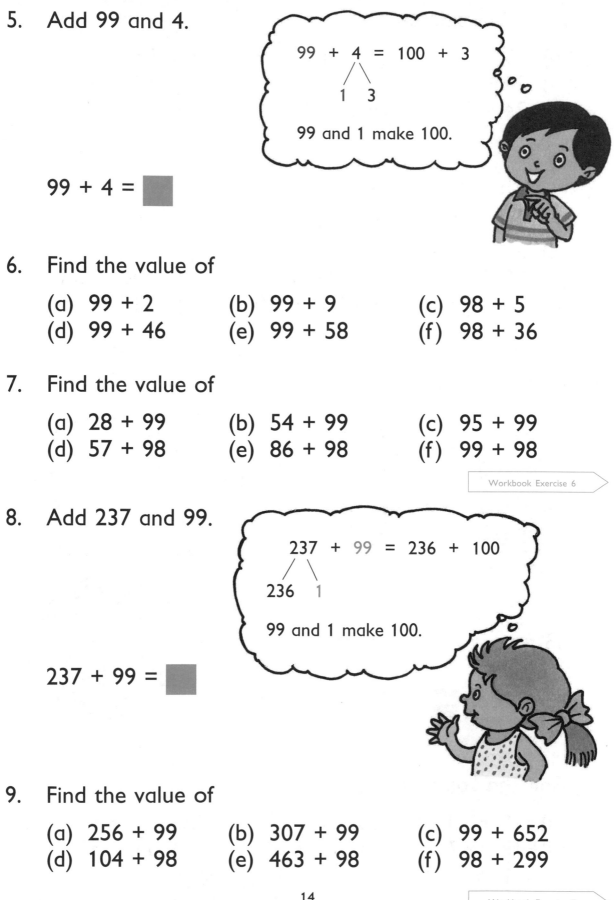

$$99 + 4 = 100 + 3$$

99 and 1 make 100.

99 + 4 = ▢

6. Find the value of

(a) 99 + 2   (b) 99 + 9   (c) 98 + 5
(d) 99 + 46   (e) 99 + 58   (f) 98 + 36

7. Find the value of

(a) 28 + 99   (b) 54 + 99   (c) 95 + 99
(d) 57 + 98   (e) 86 + 98   (f) 99 + 98

Workbook Exercise 6

8. Add 237 and 99.

$$237 + 99 = 236 + 100$$

99 and 1 make 100.

237 + 99 = ▢

9. Find the value of

(a) 256 + 99   (b) 307 + 99   (c) 99 + 652
(d) 104 + 98   (e) 463 + 98   (f) 98 + 299

Workbook Exercise 7

3 Methods for Mental Subtraction

What number is 40 less than 578?

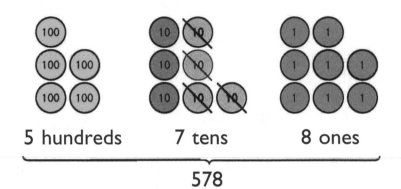

5 hundreds   7 tens   8 ones

578

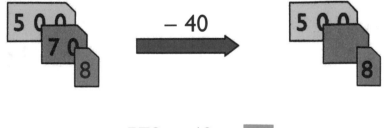

Subtract 4 tens from 578.

578 − 40 = ▊

What number is 4 less than 578?

What number is 400 less than 578?

1. Find the value of

   (a) 38 – 2   (b) 24 – 6   (c) 70 – 9
   (d) 50 – 30   (e) 70 – 20   (f) 90 – 50
   (g) 51 – 30   (h) 78 – 20   (i) 95 – 50

   Workbook Exercise 8

2. Find the value of

   (a) 230 – 7   (b) 206 – 9   (c) 411 – 8
   (d) 780 – 60   (e) 450 – 70   (f) 540 – 80
   (g) 500 – 200 (h) 700 – 400 (i) 900 – 300
   (j) 542 – 200 (k) 753 – 400 (l) 908 – 300

   Workbook Exercise 9

3. Subtract 23 from 54.

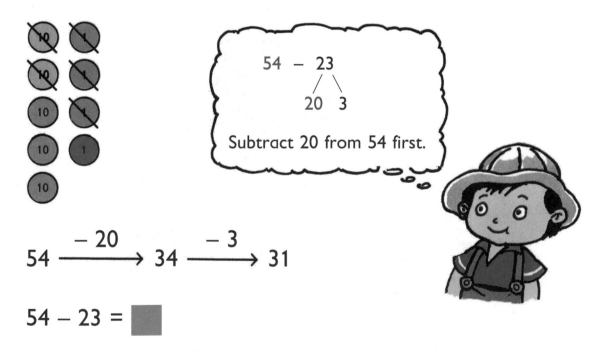

54 – 23

```
54  –20→  34  –3→  31
```

54 – 23 = ⬛

4. Find the value of

   (a) 58 – 17   (b) 87 – 16   (c) 42 – 12
   (d) 36 – 25   (e) 65 – 42   (f) 75 – 55

Workbook Exercise 10

5. Subtract 99 from 300.

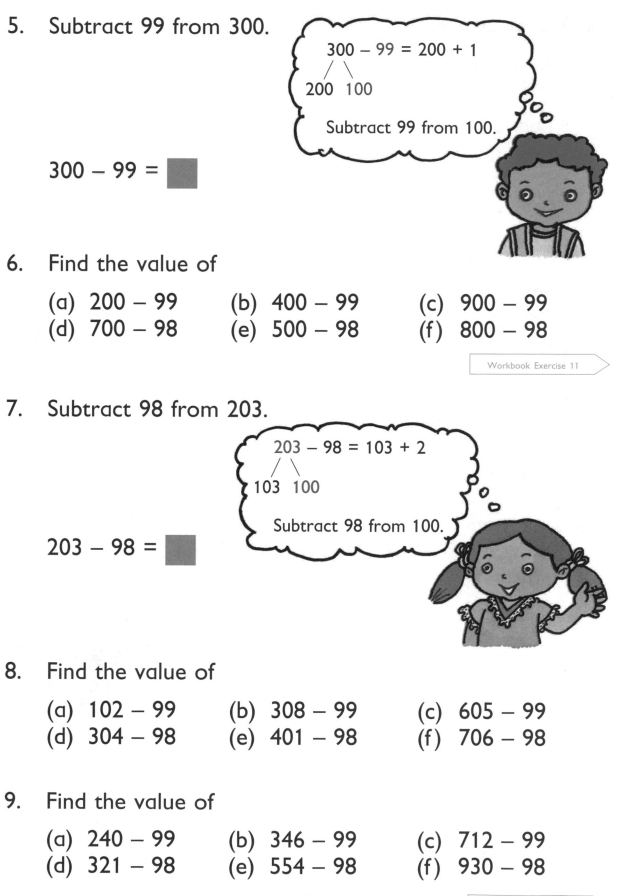

$$300 - 99 = 200 + 1$$

200 100

Subtract 99 from 100.

$300 - 99 = \boxed{}$

6. Find the value of

(a) 200 − 99   (b) 400 − 99   (c) 900 − 99
(d) 700 − 98   (e) 500 − 98   (f) 800 − 98

Workbook Exercise 11

7. Subtract 98 from 203.

$$203 - 98 = 103 + 2$$

103 100

Subtract 98 from 100.

$203 - 98 = \boxed{}$

8. Find the value of

(a) 102 − 99   (b) 308 − 99   (c) 605 − 99
(d) 304 − 98   (e) 401 − 98   (f) 706 − 98

9. Find the value of

(a) 240 − 99   (b) 346 − 99   (c) 712 − 99
(d) 321 − 98   (e) 554 − 98   (f) 930 − 98

Workbook Exercise 12

PRACTICE 1B

Find the value of each of the following:

	(a)	(b)	(c)
1.	234 + 8	365 + 80	705 + 200
2.	73 + 16	62 + 99	98 + 304
3.	105 – 7	512 – 300	420 – 80
4.	56 – 15	74 – 32	89 – 27
5.	325 – 99	406 – 98	600 – 99

6. There are 92 students in a school cafeteria.
   57 of them are boys.
   How many girls are there?

7. Alex made 185 sticks of chicken satay.
   He made 28 more sticks of beef satay than chicken satay.
   How many sticks of beef satay did he make?

8. Samy had $500.
   He bought a washing machine and had $98 left.
   Find the cost of the washing machine.

9. A rice cooker costs $64.
   It costs $15 more than a kettle.
   What is the cost of the kettle?

10. John sold 215 copies of newspapers on Saturday.
    He sold 285 copies of newspapers on Sunday.

    (a) How many copies of newspapers did he sell on both days?

    (b) How many more copies of newspapers did he sell on Sunday than on Saturday?

PRACTICE 1C

Find the value of each of the following:

(a)	(b)	(c)
1. 316 + 70	287 + 40	153 + 57
2. 185 + 65	333 + 78	425 + 75
3. 409 + 98	176 + 54	399 + 99
4. 751 − 20	505 − 50	214 − 36
5. 400 − 198	422 − 63	600 − 98

6. (a) What number is 5 more than 299?
   (b) What number is 7 less than 406?

7. After using 255 eggs to make cakes,
   Mrs. Ward had 45 eggs left.
   How many eggs did she have at first?

8. John is 135 cm tall.
   He is 29 cm shorter than David.
   Find David's height.

9. There were 98 boys and 86 girls at a concert.
   There were 40 more children than adults.

   (a) How many children were there?
   (b) How many adults were there?

10. Ian had 200 kg of cherries.
    He sold 86 kg on the first day and 54 kg on the
    second day.
    (a) How many kilograms of cherries did he sell
        altogether?
    (b) How many kilograms of cherries had he left?

Multiplication and Division

1 Multiplying and Dividing by 4

Count the stickers by fours.

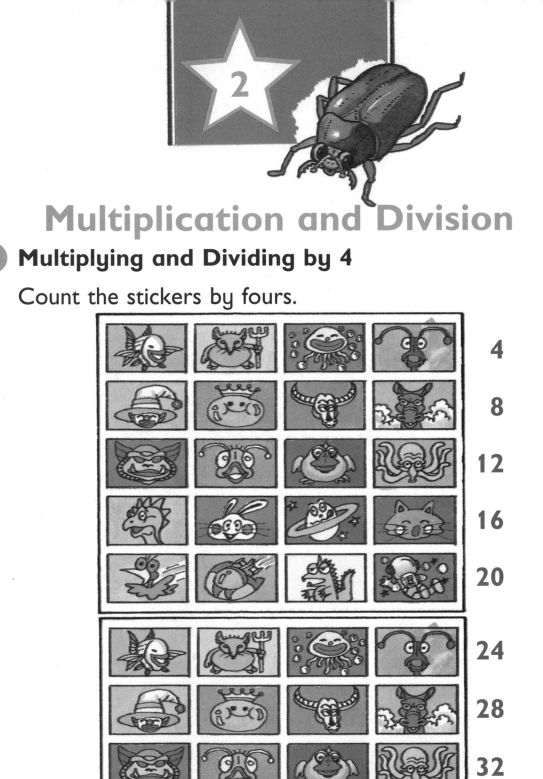

4

8

12

16

20

24

28

32

36

40

There are 4 stickers in each row.

(a) How many stickers are there in 3 rows?

Count by fours:
4, 8, 12

$4 \times 3 = \boxed{}$

There are $\boxed{}$ stickers in 3 rows.

(b) How many stickers are there in 7 rows?

Count by fours:
4, 8, 12, 16, 20,
24, 28

$4 \times 7 = \boxed{}$

There are $\boxed{}$ stickers in 7 rows.

1. (a) Multiply 4 by 4.

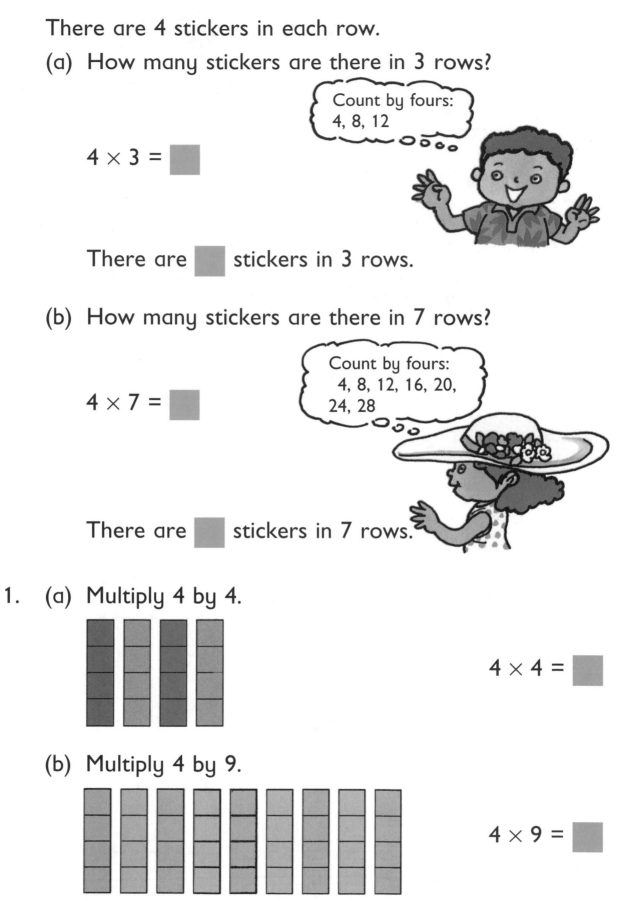

$4 \times 4 = \boxed{}$

(b) Multiply 4 by 9.

$4 \times 9 = \boxed{}$

21

2.

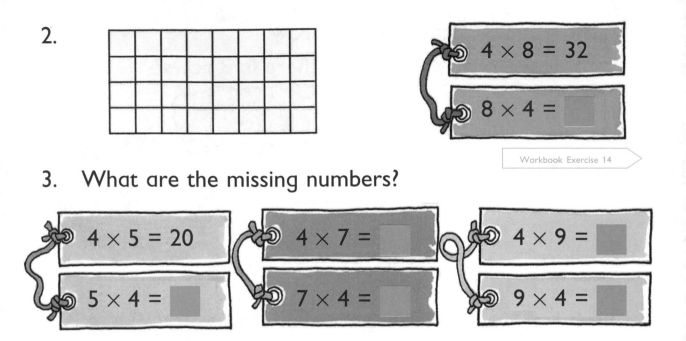

Workbook Exercise 14

3. What are the missing numbers?

$4 \times 5 = 20$

$5 \times 4 = $

$4 \times 7 = $

$7 \times 4 = $

$4 \times 9 = $

$9 \times 4 = $

4. Complete the number sentences.

$4 \times 1 = 4$

$4 \times 2 = 8$

$4 \times 3 = $

$4 \times 4 = $

$4 \times 5 = $

$4 \times 6 = $

$4 \times 7 = $

$4 \times 8 = $

$4 \times 9 = $

$4 \times 10 = $

$1 \times 4 = 4$

$2 \times 4 = $

$3 \times 4 = $

$4 \times 4 = $

$5 \times 4 = $

$6 \times 4 = $

$7 \times 4 = $

$8 \times 4 = $

$9 \times 4 = $

$10 \times 4 = $

5.

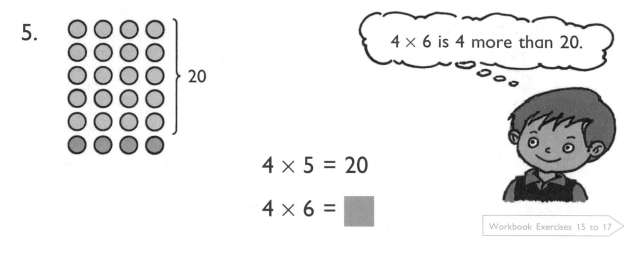

$4 \times 5 = 20$

$4 \times 6 = \boxed{}$

Workbook Exercises 15 to 17

6. (a) Divide 12 tomatoes into 4 equal groups.
   How many tomatoes are there in each group?

$12 \div 4 = \boxed{}$

There are $\boxed{}$ tomatoes in each group.

(b) Divide 12 tomatoes into groups of 4.
   How many groups are there?

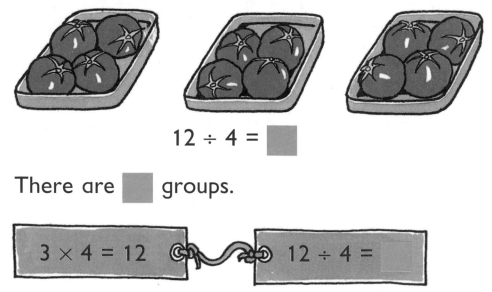

$12 \div 4 = \boxed{}$

There are $\boxed{}$ groups.

$3 \times 4 = 12$ ⟿ $12 \div 4 = \boxed{}$

23

7. What are the missing numbers?

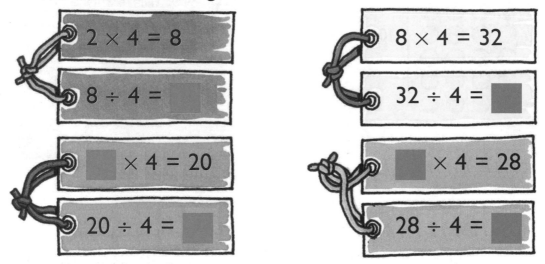

$2 \times 4 = 8$

$8 \div 4 = \boxed{}$

$\boxed{} \times 4 = 20$

$20 \div 4 = \boxed{}$

$8 \times 4 = 32$

$32 \div 4 = \boxed{}$

$\boxed{} \times 4 = 28$

$28 \div 4 = \boxed{}$

8. Find the value of

(a) $4 \div 4 = \boxed{}$ (b) $16 \div 4 = \boxed{}$ (c) $36 \div 4 = \boxed{}$

(d) $24 \div 4 = \boxed{}$ (e) $12 \div 4 = \boxed{}$ (f) $40 \div 4 = \boxed{}$

9. Suhua saves the same amount of money every day.

   (a) If she saves \$32 in 4 days, how much does she save a day?

   $$32 \div 4 = \boxed{}$$

   She saves \$ $\boxed{}$ a day.

   (b) If she saves \$4 a day, how many days does she take to save \$40?

   $$40 \div 4 = \boxed{}$$

   She takes $\boxed{}$ days to save \$40.

24

PRACTICE 2A

Find the value of each of the following:

	(a)	(b)	(c)
1.	3×4	7×4	2×4
2.	$4 \div 4$	$32 \div 4$	$16 \div 4$
3.	4×6	4×10	4×8
4.	$8 \div 4$	$20 \div 4$	$40 \div 4$
5.	$36 \div 4$	$12 \div 4$	$24 \div 4$

6. A taxi can carry 4 passengers.
   How many passengers can 5 taxis carry?

7. Mr. Baker packs 16 kg of coffee powder equally into 4 bags.
   How many kilograms of coffee powder are there in each bag?

8. 6 children went to a library.
   Each child borrowed 4 books.
   How many books did they borrow altogether?

9. Mr. Rogers bought 4 T-shirts for $40.
   How much did one T-shirt cost?

10. Miss Wells made 4 sets of cushion covers.
    She used 8 m of cloth for each set.
    How many meters of cloth did she use altogether?

11. There are 36 glasses in 4 boxes.
    There are the same number of glasses in each box.
    How many glasses are there in each box?

② Multiplying and Dividing by 5

Count the picture cards by fives.

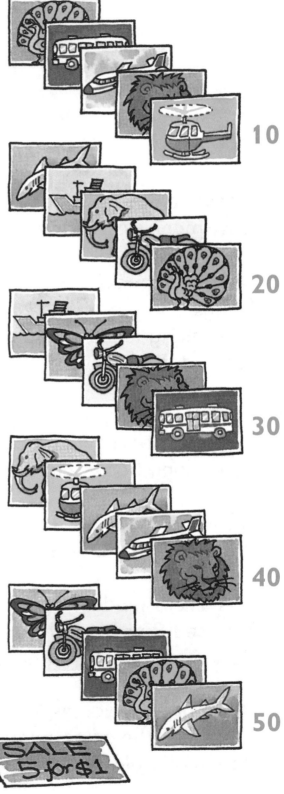

1. At a sale, picture cards were sold at 5 for $1.

   (a) Sara bought some picture cards for $3.
   How many picture cards did she buy?

   $5 \times 3 = $

   Count by fives:
   5, 10, 15

   She bought ☐ picture cards.

   (b) Dani bought some picture cards for $8.
   How many picture cards did she buy?

   $5 \times 8 = $ ☐

   Count by fives:
   5, 10, 15, 20,
   25, 30, 35, 40

   She bought ☐ picture cards.

Workbook Exercise 19

2. Russell bought 9 five-cent stamps.
   How much did he pay?

   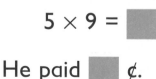

   Count by fives:
   5, 10, 15, 20, 25, 30,
   35, 40, 45

   $5 \times 9 = $ ☐

   He paid ¢.

3. How much money is there in each set?

(a)

(b)

4. What are the missing numbers?

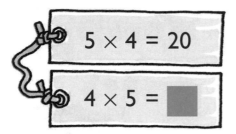
$5 \times 4 = 20$
$4 \times 5 = $ ▣

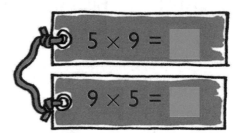
$5 \times 9 = $ ▣
$9 \times 5 = $ ▣

5. Find the value of

(a) 7×5 (b) 6×5 (c) 1×5
(d) 5×5 (e) 5×2 (f) 10×5

Workbook Exercise 20

6. What are the missing numbers?

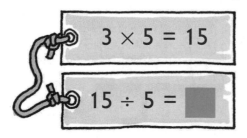
$3 \times 5 = 15$
$15 \div 5 = $ ▣

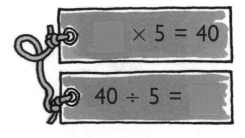
▢ $\times 5 = 40$
$40 \div 5 = $ ▣

7. Find the value of

(a) $30 \div 5$ (b) $5 \div 5$ (c) $25 \div 5$
(d) $10 \div 5$ (e) $50 \div 5$ (f) $45 \div 5$

Workbook Exercise 21

PRACTICE 2B

Find the value of each of the following:

	(a)	(b)	(c)
1.	5 × 5	4 × 5	7 × 5
2.	15 ÷ 5	25 ÷ 5	5 ÷ 5
3.	5 × 1	5 × 9	5 × 3
4.	20 ÷ 5	30 ÷ 5	45 ÷ 5
5.	40 ÷ 5	50 ÷ 5	35 ÷ 5

6. Mrs. Larson bought 5 kg of prawns.
   1 kg of prawns cost $8.
   How much did she pay for the prawns?

7. A baker sold 5 chocolate cakes a day.
   Each chocolate cake cost $7.
   How much money did he receive?

8. 5 people spent $45 for lunch together.
   They shared the cost of the lunch equally.
   How much did each person spend?

9. Jamie packed 25 cookies into packets of 5.
   How many packets of cookies did she get?

10. Carlos bought 3 kg of grapes.
    How much did he pay?

$5 for 1 kg

GRAPES

11. Lindsey paid $30 for 5 kg of clams.
    What was the cost of 1 kg of clams?

3 Multiplying and Dividing by 10

Count the eggs by tens.

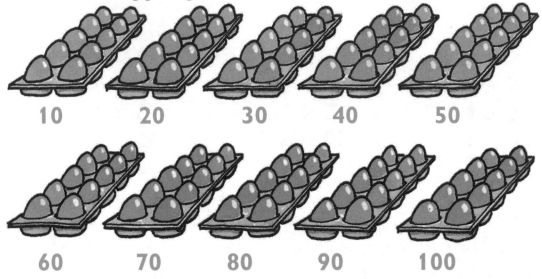

10	20	30	40	50

60	70	80	90	100

1. In a supermarket, eggs were sold in trays of 10 each.

   (a) Lindsey bought 4 trays of eggs.
   How many eggs did she buy?

   $10 \times 4 = \boxed{}$

   Count by tens:
   10, 20, 30, 40

   She bought $\boxed{}$ eggs.

   (b) Michelle bought 6 trays of eggs.
   How many eggs did she buy?

   $10 \times 6 = \boxed{}$

   Count by tens:
   10, 20, 30, 40, 50, 60

   She bought $\boxed{}$ eggs.

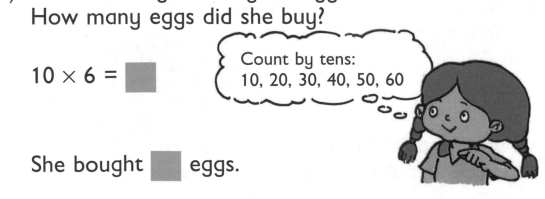

2. How much money is there in each set?

(a)

(b)

3. What are the missing numbers?

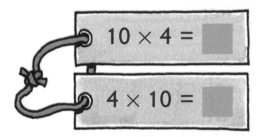
$10 \times 4 = \boxed{}$

$4 \times 10 = \boxed{}$

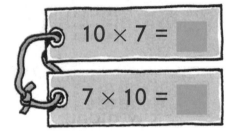
$10 \times 7 = \boxed{}$

$7 \times 10 = \boxed{}$

4. Find the value of

(a) 10×3 (b) 10×10 (c) 10×9
(d) 2×10 (e) 1×10 (f) 6×10

Workbook Exercise 22

5. What are the missing numbers?

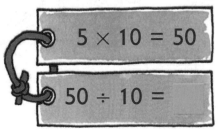
$5 \times 10 = 50$

$50 \div 10 = \boxed{}$

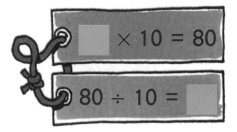
$\boxed{} \times 10 = 80$

$80 \div 10 = \boxed{}$

6. Find the value of

(a) $60 \div 10$ (b) $30 \div 10$ (c) $10 \div 10$
(d) $40 \div 10$ (e) $100 \div 10$ (f) $90 \div 10$

Workbook Exercise 23

PRACTICE 2C

Find the value of each of the following:

	(a)	(b)	(c)
1.	4 × 10	1 × 10	7 × 10
2.	60 ÷ 10	20 ÷ 10	70 ÷ 10
3.	10 × 6	10 × 5	10 × 10
4.	30 ÷ 10	10 ÷ 10	90 ÷ 10
5.	100 ÷ 10	80 ÷ 10	50 ÷ 10

6. Mrs. Wells bought 10 concert tickets.
   Each concert ticket cost $7.
   How much did she pay altogether?

7. Emily bought 40 beads.
   The beads were sold in packets of 10.
   How many packets of beads did Emily buy?

8. Dani made 10 jars of pineapple jam.
   She sold them at $3 for one jar.
   How much money did she receive?

9. Maria paid $80 for 10 cans of paint.
   Find the cost of one can of paint.

10. Kristin bought 10 packets of sugar.
    Each packet weighed 5 kg.
    How many kilograms of sugar did she buy?

11. In a supermarket, eggs were sold in trays of 10.
    Mrs. Ward bought 60 eggs.
    How many trays of eggs did she buy?

PRACTICE 2D

Find the value of each of the following:

	(a)	(b)	(c)
1.	6 × 4	2 × 10	6 × 5
2.	12 ÷ 4	40 ÷ 10	20 ÷ 5
3.	4 × 8	5 × 5	9 × 4
4.	40 ÷ 5	28 ÷ 4	35 ÷ 5
5.	9 × 5	10 × 3	8 × 10

6. Ashley paid $36 for 4 m of cloth.
   Find the cost of 1 m of cloth.

7. A tailor made 5 dresses.
   He used 3 m of cloth for each dress.
   How many meters of cloth did he use altogether?

8. A jigsaw puzzle costs $10.
   How many jigsaw puzzles can Matthew buy with $50?

9. 24 chairs are arranged equally in 4 rows.
   How many chairs are there in each row?

10. Mrs. Holt packed 40 pies into boxes of 5 each.
    How many boxes of pies were there?

11. Joe bought 8 packets of greeting cards.
    There were 4 greeting cards in each packet.
    How many greeting cards were there altogether?

PRACTICE 2E

Find the value of each of the following:

	(a)	(b)	(c)
1.	3 × 4	5 × 8	9 × 10
2.	20 ÷ 4	50 ÷ 10	25 ÷ 5
3.	4 × 9	10 × 7	4 × 4
4.	30 ÷ 5	32 ÷ 4	10 ÷ 10
5.	10 × 10	4 × 7	5 × 3

6. Lindsey used 20 m of material to make curtains.
   She used 4 m of material for each set of curtains.
   How many sets of curtains did she make?

7. Dani packed 50 cupcakes equally into 5 boxes.
   How many cupcakes were there in each box?

8. Tracy bought 6 trays of eggs.
   There were 10 eggs in each tray.
   How many eggs did she buy altogether?

9. Pablo spent $40 on lychees.
   How many kilograms of lychees did he buy?

$4 for 1 kg

LYCHEES

10. 36 scouts went camping.
    Each group of 4 scouts shared a tent.
    How many tents were there?

11. Carlos and John shared $16 equally.
    How much money did each boy receive?

REVIEW A

Find the value of each of the following:

	(a)	(b)	(c)
1.	781 + 19	250 + 398	608 + 294
2.	266 − 6	502 − 493	700 − 299
3.	6 × 2	5 × 6	7 × 10
4.	40 ÷ 4	18 ÷ 3	45 ÷ 5

5. 1000 people were invited to an exhibition.
   Only 958 of them turned up at the exhibition.
   How many people did **not** turn up?

6. Mrs. Owens sold 105 eggs on Monday morning.
   She sold 95 eggs on Monday afternoon.
   Find the total number of eggs she sold on Monday.

7. Mrs. Brown paid $35 for some jars of honey.
   How many jars of honey did she buy?

$5 for
1 jar

8. A box of 10 glasses cost $9.
   Mrs. Gray bought 50 glasses.
   (a) How many boxes of glasses did
       she buy?
   (b) How much did she pay?

$488

9. The television set costs $85 less than
   the oven.
   (a) Find the cost of the televsion set.
   (b) Find the total cost of the television
       set and the oven.

35

Money

1 Dollars and Cents

Sara paid this amount of money for a book.

10, 15, 16, 17, 18 dollars
50, 60, 65 cents

The book cost $18.65.

$18.65

Eighteen dollars and sixty-five cents

$18.65 is 18 dollars and 65 cents.
The dot • separates the cents from the dollars.

1. How much money is there in each set?

(a)

(b)

(c)

(d)

2. Read the prices of these items.

Workbook Exercise 24

3. Write in dollars and cents.

(a) $4.75 = ▢ dollars ▢ cents

(b) $8.00 = ▢ dollars ▢ cents

(c) $0.35 = ▢ dollars ▢ cents

Workbook Exercises 25 & 26

4. (a) How many one-cent coins can be changed for $1?

(b) How many ten-cent coins can be changed for $1?

(c) How many five-cent coins can be changed for $1?

5. (a)

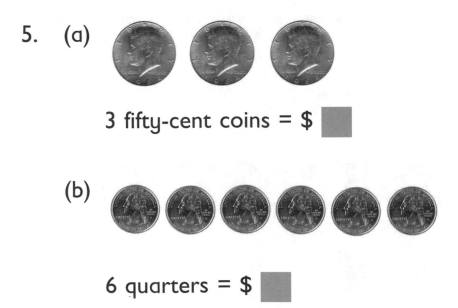

3 fifty-cent coins = $ ▢

(b)

6 quarters = $ ▢

38

6. (a) How many quarters can be changed for a
         one-dollar bill?
    (b) How many five-dollar bills can be changed for a
         twenty-dollar bill?

7.

I have 3 five-dollar bills
and 8 one-dollar bills.

Melissa

How much money does Melissa have?

9. Write in dollars.

    (a)   65¢ = $ ▨

    (b) 165¢ = $ ▨

$1 = 100¢

9. Write in cents.

    (a) $0.85 = ▨ ¢

    (b) $1.20 = ▨ ¢

    (c) $2.00 = ▨ ¢

    (d) $2.05 = ▨ ¢

Workbook Exercise 27

10. Suhua bought the ruler.
    She gave the shopkeeper $1.
    How much change did she receive?

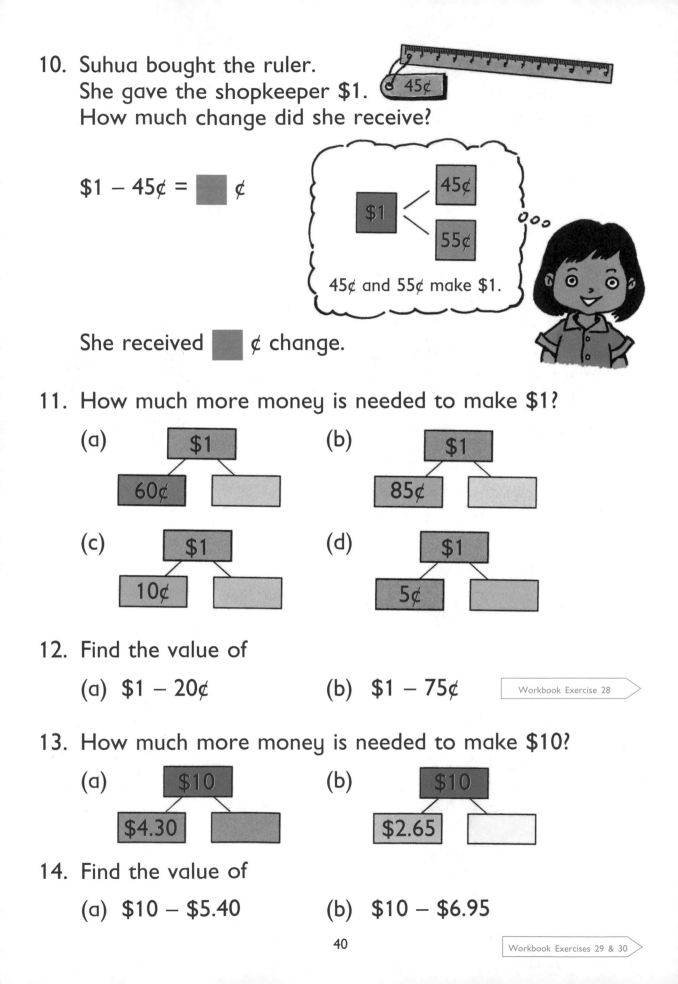

$1 – 45¢ = ☐ ¢

$1
45¢
55¢

45¢ and 55¢ make $1.

She received ☐ ¢ change.

11. How much more money is needed to make $1?

(a)
$1
60¢

(b)
$1
85¢

(c)
$1
10¢

(d)
$1
5¢

12. Find the value of

(a) $1 – 20¢

(b) $1 – 75¢

Workbook Exercise 28

13. How much more money is needed to make $10?

(a)
$10
$4.30

(b)
$10
$2.65

14. Find the value of

(a) $10 – $5.40

(b) $10 – $6.95

Workbook Exercises 29 & 30

PRACTICE 3A

1. Write in dollars and cents.

   (a) $3.45 = ▮ dollars ▮ cents

   (b) $6.00 = ▮ dollars ▮ cents

   (c) $7.05 = ▮ dollars ▮ cents

   (d) $0.80 = ▮ dollars ▮ cents

2. Write in cents.

   (a) $2.20 = ▮ ¢   (b) $3.05 = ▮ ¢

3. Write in dollars.

   (a) 75¢ = $ ▮   (b) 260¢ = $ ▮

4. (a) How many quarters can be changed for a one-dollar bill?

   (b) How many five-dollar bills can be changed for a twenty-dollar bill?

   (c) How many twenty-dollar bills can be changed for a hundred-dollar bill?

5. Matthew bought a file for 85¢.
   He gave the cashier $1.
   How much change did he receive?

6. Amber wants to buy this teddy bear.
   She has only $8.60.
   How much more money does she need?

$10

41

Adding Money

Lauren bought an umbrella for $4.15 and a T-shirt for $3.50.
How much did she spend altogether?

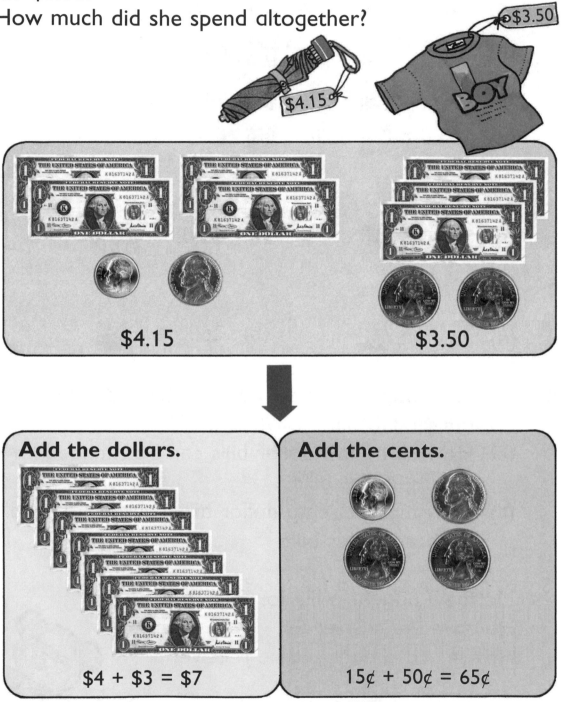

$4.15

$3.50

Add the dollars.

$4 + $3 = $7

Add the cents.

15¢ + 50¢ = 65¢

$4.15 + $3.50 = $ ▮

She spent $ ▮ altogether.

1. (a) $4.95 + $2 = $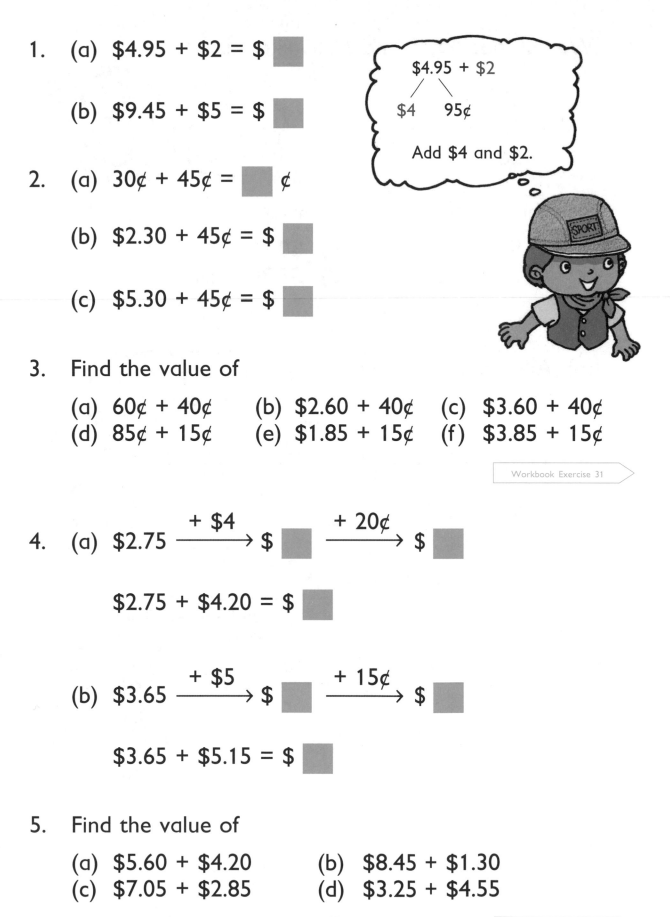

    (b) $9.45 + $5 = $

2. (a) 30¢ + 45¢ = ▢ ¢

    (b) $2.30 + 45¢ = $

    (c) $5.30 + 45¢ = $

$4.95 + $2

$4   95¢

Add $4 and $2.

3. Find the value of

    (a) 60¢ + 40¢   (b) $2.60 + 40¢   (c) $3.60 + 40¢
    (d) 85¢ + 15¢   (e) $1.85 + 15¢   (f) $3.85 + 15¢

Workbook Exercise 31

4. (a) $2.75 $\xrightarrow{\text{+ \$4}}$ $ ▢ $\xrightarrow{\text{+ 20¢}}$ $ ▢

    $2.75 + $4.20 = $ ▢

    (b) $3.65 $\xrightarrow{\text{+ \$5}}$ $ ▢ $\xrightarrow{\text{+ 15¢}}$ $ ▢

    $3.65 + $5.15 = $ ▢

5. Find the value of

    (a) $5.60 + $4.20   (b) $8.45 + $1.30
    (c) $7.05 + $2.85   (d) $3.25 + $4.55

Workbook Exercise 32

6. We can add $3.45 and $2.65 like this:

$$\begin{array}{r} \$3.45 \\ + \ \$2.65 \\ \hline \$6.10 \end{array}$$

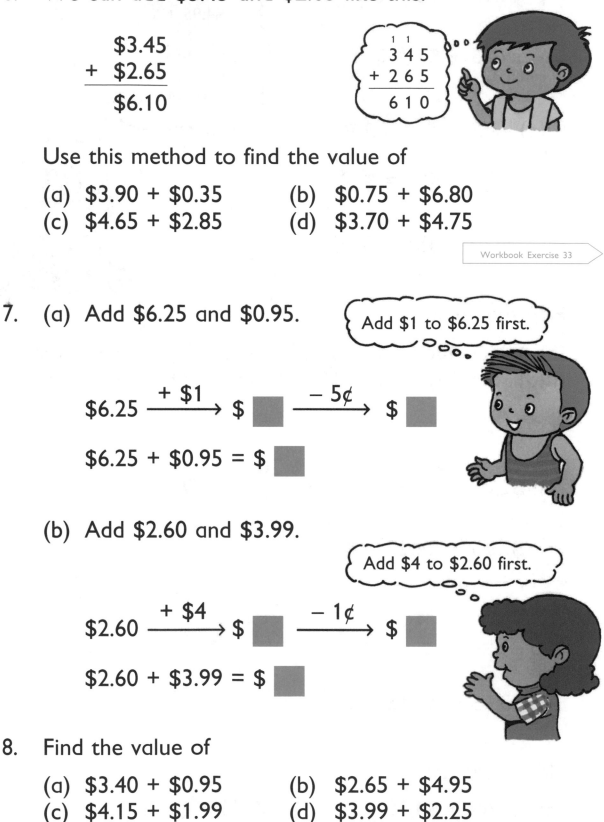

$$\begin{array}{r} {\scriptstyle 1 \ 1} \\ 3\ 4\ 5 \\ + \ 2\ 6\ 5 \\ \hline 6\ 1\ 0 \end{array}$$

Use this method to find the value of

(a) $3.90 + $0.35   (b) $0.75 + $6.80
(c) $4.65 + $2.85   (d) $3.70 + $4.75

Workbook Exercise 33

7. (a) Add $6.25 and $0.95.

Add $1 to $6.25 first.

$6.25 $\xrightarrow{+ \$1}$ $ ▢ $\xrightarrow{- 5¢}$ $ ▢

$6.25 + $0.95 = $ ▢

(b) Add $2.60 and $3.99.

Add $4 to $2.60 first.

$2.60 $\xrightarrow{+ \$4}$ $ ▢ $\xrightarrow{- 1¢}$ $ ▢

$2.60 + $3.99 = $ ▢

8. Find the value of

(a) $3.40 + $0.95   (b) $2.65 + $4.95
(c) $4.15 + $1.99   (d) $3.99 + $2.25

Workbook Exercise 34

9. After paying for a set meal which cost $5.95,
   David had $1.60 left.
   How much money did he have at first?

$5.95 + $1.60 = ▮

He had $ ▮ at first.

10. A toy car cost $5.70.
    A stuffed toy cost $3.80 more than the toy car.
    How much did the stuffed toy cost?

$5.70 + $3.80 = ▮

The stuffed toy cost $ ▮ .

3 Subtracting Money

Nicole has $8.75.
She buys a jumping rope for $3.50.
How much money has she left?

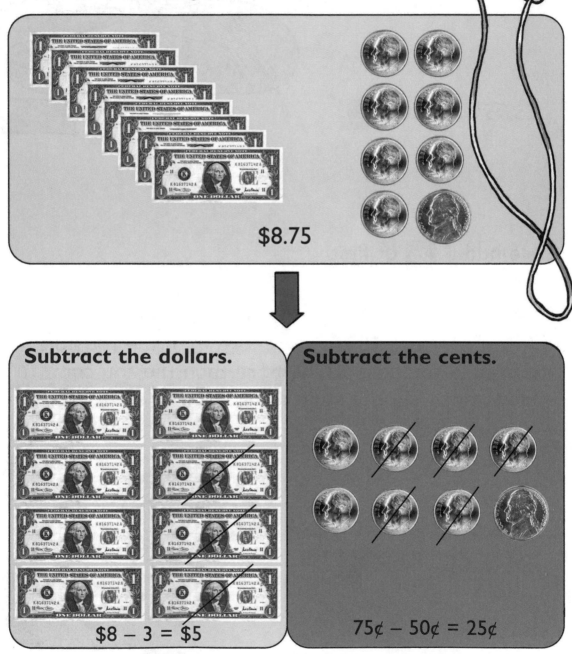

$8.75

Subtract the dollars.

$8 − 3 = $5

Subtract the cents.

75¢ − 50¢ = 25¢

$8.75 − $3.50 = $ ◻

She has $ ◻ left.

1. Find the value of
   (a) $8.15 - $3   (b) $6.35 - $2   (c) $4.80 - $4
   (d) 60¢ - 15¢   (e) $2.60 - 15¢   (f) $3.60 - 15¢

2. (a) $1 - 40¢ = 60¢

   (b) $3 - 40¢ = $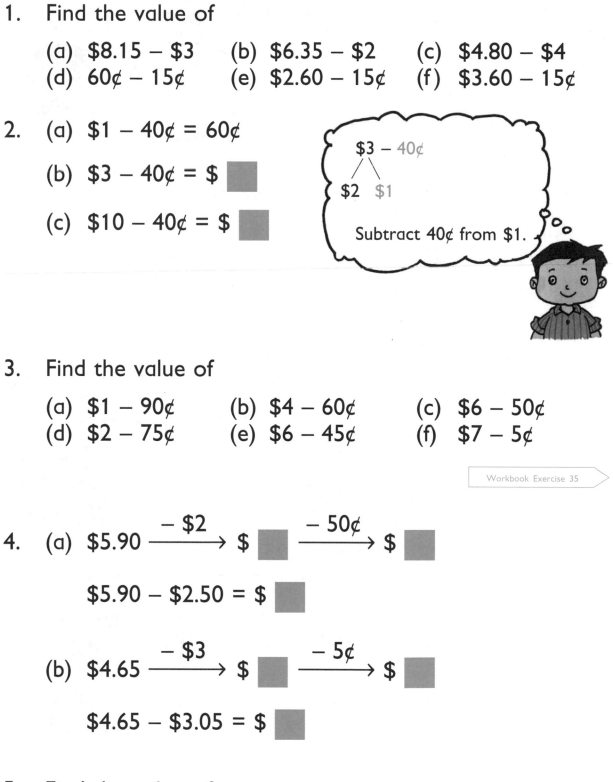

   (c) $10 - 40¢ = $

   $3 - 40¢

   $2 $1

   Subtract 40¢ from $1.

3. Find the value of
   (a) $1 - 90¢   (b) $4 - 60¢   (c) $6 - 50¢
   (d) $2 - 75¢   (e) $6 - 45¢   (f) $7 - 5¢

Workbook Exercise 35

4. (a) $5.90 ──── $2 ────→ $ ──── 50¢ ────→ $

   $5.90 - $2.50 = $

   (b) $4.65 ──── $3 ────→ $ ──── 5¢ ────→ $

   $4.65 - $3.05 = $

5. Find the value of
   (a) $8.60 - $2.40   (b) $4.85 - $1.30
   (c) $6.45 - $6.05   (d) $8.70 - $4.55

Workbook Exercise 36

6. We can subtract $3.75 from $5.35 like this:

$$\begin{array}{r} \$5.35 \\ - \ \$3.75 \\ \hline \$1.60 \end{array}$$

Use this method to find the value of

(a) $5.65 − $0.85   (b) $4.10 − $0.45
(c) $3.00 − $0.35   (d) $8.00 − $3.70
(e) $6.25 − $4.65   (f) $7.50 − $5.85

Workbook Exercise 37

7. (a) Subtract $0.95 from $4.60.

Subtract $1 from $4.60 first.

$$\$4.60 \xrightarrow{\ -\ \$1\ } \$ \ \blacksquare \ \xrightarrow{\ +\ 5\cancel{c}\ } \$ \ \blacksquare$$

$4.60 − $0.95 = $ ■

(b) Subtract $2.99 from $6.25.

Subtract $3 from $6.25 first.

$$\$6.25 \xrightarrow{\ -\ \$3\ } \$ \ \blacksquare \ \xrightarrow{\ +\ 1\cancel{c}\ } \$ \ \blacksquare$$

$6.25 − $2.99 = $ ■

8. Find the value of

(a) $3.45 − $0.95   (b) $4.30 − $1.95
(c) $6.20 − $2.99   (d) $5.00 − $3.99

48

Workbook Exercise 38

9. Mary bought a doll which cost $8.45.
   She gave the cashier $10.
   How much change did she receive?

$8.45

$10 − $8.45 = $ [ ]

She received $ [ ] change.

10. A box of cookies costs $4.75.
    A box of chocolates costs $8.20.
    How much cheaper is the box of cookies?

$8.20 − $4.75 = $ [ ]

The box of cookies is $ [ ] cheaper.

PRACTICE 3B

Find the value of each of the following:

	(a)	(b)
1.	$4.40 + $1.60	$0.80 − $0.45
2.	$2.80 + $3.15	$6.55 − $2.50
3.	$5.35 + $3.70	$7.05 − $5.25
4.	$7.70 + $1.75	$4.30 − $2.75
5.	$3.60 + $4.99	$8.10 − $4.95

6. Find the total cost of the birdie and the racket.

$1.40

$7.85

7. A pair of shoes costs $10.
   A pair of slippers costs $6.30.
   How much cheaper is the pair of slippers?

8. Eric bought a greeting card for $1.85.
   He gave the cashier $5.
   How much change did he receive?

9. Emily has $4.25.
   Mitchell has $1.95 more than Emily.
   How much money does Mitchell have?

10. Taylor has $5.65.
    Her mother gives her $1.70 more.
    How much money does Taylor have now?

PRACTICE 3C

Find the value of each of the following:

	(a)	(b)
1.	$3.65 + $6.35	$0.90 − $0.55
2.	$4.20 + $5.15	$3.35 − $1.45
3.	$6.75 + $2.80	$8.00 − $6.70
4.	$8.35 + $1.85	$4.35 − $2.70
5.	$7.80 + $1.95	$9.05 − $8.99

6. After paying $6.80 for a shirt, Ali had $2.40 left.
   How much money did he have at first?

7. Devi bought the can of sardines and the can of beans.
   How much did she spend altogether?

8. Carlos saved $6.45 in two weeks.
   He saved $3.95 in the first week.
   How much did he save in the second week?

9. Ryan had $8.05.
   After buying a belt, he had $1.90 left.
   How much did the belt cost?

10. Sara had $9.20.
    She spent $2.80 on a T-shirt.
    How much money had she left?

Fractions

① Halves and Quarters

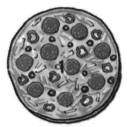

a whole

halves

Divide a circle into 2 equal parts.
Each part is a **half** circle.

Divide a circle into 4 equal parts.
Each part is a **quarter** circle.

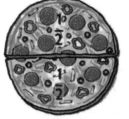

quarters

Which is greater, $\frac{1}{2}$ or $\frac{1}{4}$?

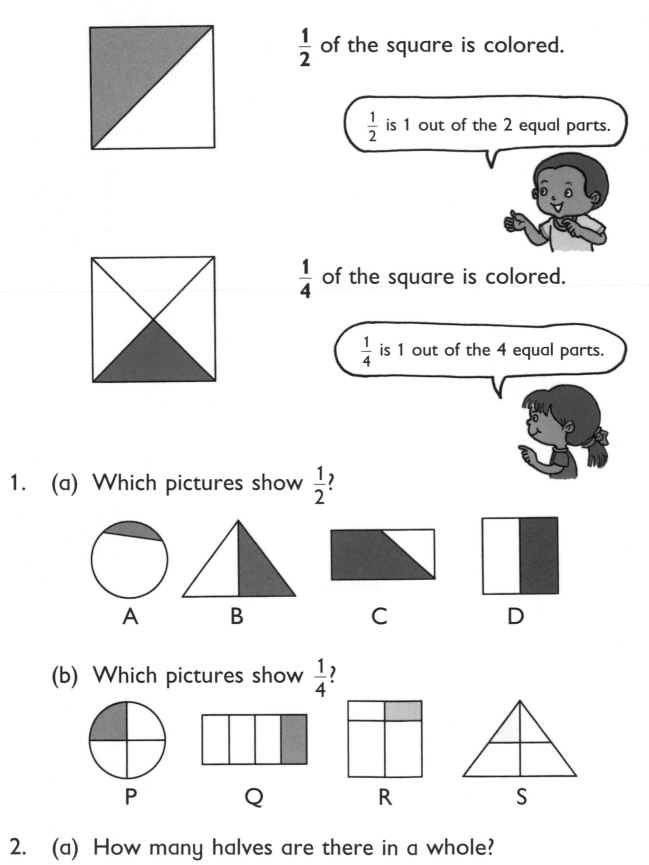

$\frac{1}{2}$ of the square is colored.

$\frac{1}{2}$ is 1 out of the 2 equal parts.

$\frac{1}{4}$ of the square is colored.

$\frac{1}{4}$ is 1 out of the 4 equal parts.

1. (a) Which pictures show $\frac{1}{2}$?

A   B   C   D

(b) Which pictures show $\frac{1}{4}$?

P   Q   R   S

2. (a) How many halves are there in a whole?

(b) How many quarters are there in a whole?

53

Workbook Exercise 40

❷ Writing Fractions

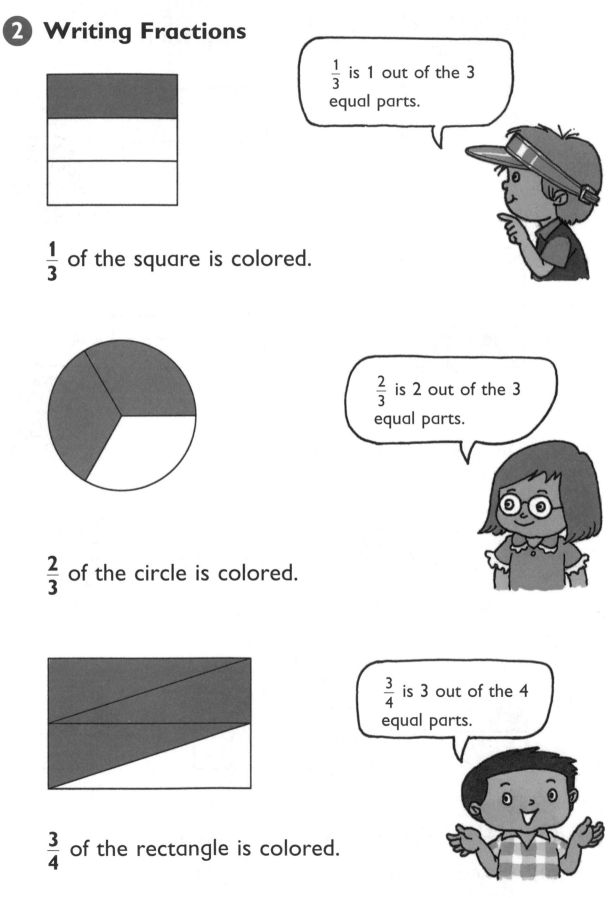

$\frac{1}{3}$ is 1 out of the 3 equal parts.

$\frac{1}{3}$ of the square is colored.

$\frac{2}{3}$ is 2 out of the 3 equal parts.

$\frac{2}{3}$ of the circle is colored.

$\frac{3}{4}$ is 3 out of the 4 equal parts.

$\frac{3}{4}$ of the rectangle is colored.

1. (a)

$\frac{1}{5}$ of the shape is colored.

$\frac{1}{5}$ is ☐ out of the ☐ equal

parts.

(b)

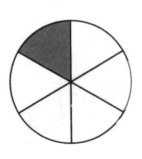

$\frac{4}{5}$ of the shape is colored.

$\frac{4}{5}$ is ☐ out of the ☐ equal

parts.

2. (a)

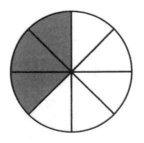

1 out of the 6 equal parts is colored.

☐ of the circle is colored.

(b)

☐ out of the ☐ equal parts are colored.

☐ of the circle is colored.

3. (a)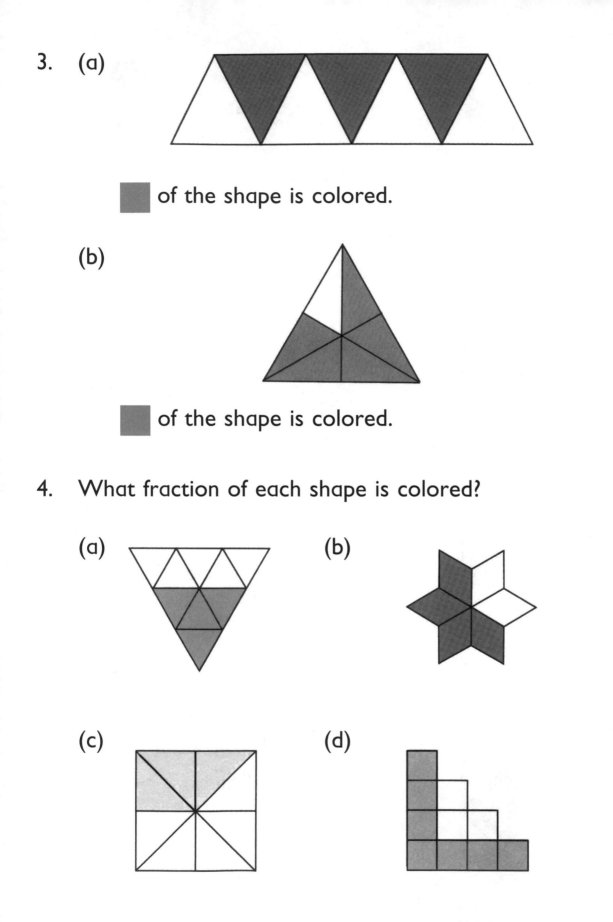

■ of the shape is colored.

(b)

■ of the shape is colored.

4. What fraction of each shape is colored?

(a)

(b)

(c)

(d)

56

5. Which is greater, $\frac{1}{4}$ or $\frac{1}{5}$?

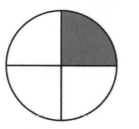 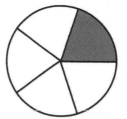

6. Arrange the fractions in order.
    Begin with the smallest.

Workbook Exercise 44

7. (a)

$\frac{3}{5}$ and [ ] make 1 whole.

(b)

$\frac{1}{7}$ and [ ] make 1 whole.

(c)

$\frac{2}{9}$ and [ ] make 1 whole.

57

Workbook Exercise 45

REVIEW B

Find the value of each of the following:

	(a)	(b)	(c)
1.	786 + 47	215 + 85	109 + 314 + 56
2.	563 − 58	400 − 299	610 − 483
3.	6 × 4	10 × 5	3 × 8
4.	16 ÷ 4	18 ÷ 2	90 ÷ 10

5. John is 132 cm tall.
   Peter is 119 cm tall.
   How much taller is John than Peter?

6. Juan had $800.
   After buying a television set, he had $398 left.
   What was the cost of the television set?

7. Jordan saves $3 a week.
   How much money does he save in 5 weeks?

8.

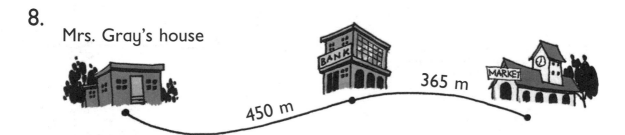

Mrs. Gray walked from her house to the bank and
then to the market.
How far did she walk?

9. John bought a packet of nuts for $2.45.
   He gave the cashier $5.
   How much change did he receive?

REVIEW C

Find the value of each of the following:

	(a)	(b)	(c)
1.	526 + 36	299 + 98	236 + 145 + 67
2.	342 − 73	300 − 69	405 − 386
3.	7 × 5	9 × 10	8 × 4
4.	45 ÷ 5	15 ÷ 3	24 ÷ 4

5. (a) What number is 9 more than 199?
   (b) What number is 50 more than 480?
   (c) What number is 8 less than 202?
   (d) What number is 30 less than 313?

6. There are 520 boys and 485 girls in a school.
   How many more boys than girls are there?

7. Peter collected 735 stamps.
   He collected 65 fewer stamps than Dan.
   How many stamps did Dan collect?

8. Mr. Beam had 27 kg of cherries.
   He packed the cherries into bags of 3 kg each.
   How many bags of cherries did he have?

9. Pablo has 6 pieces of rope.
   Each piece of rope is 5 m long.
   What is the total length of the 6 pieces of rope?

10. Matthew bought 6 packs of batteries.
    There were 4 batteries in each pack.
    How many batteries were there altogether?

Time

1 Telling Time

Mr. Lee's family has dinner at 7:05 p.m.
What time do you have dinner?

7:00

7 o'clock

7:05

5 minutes past 7

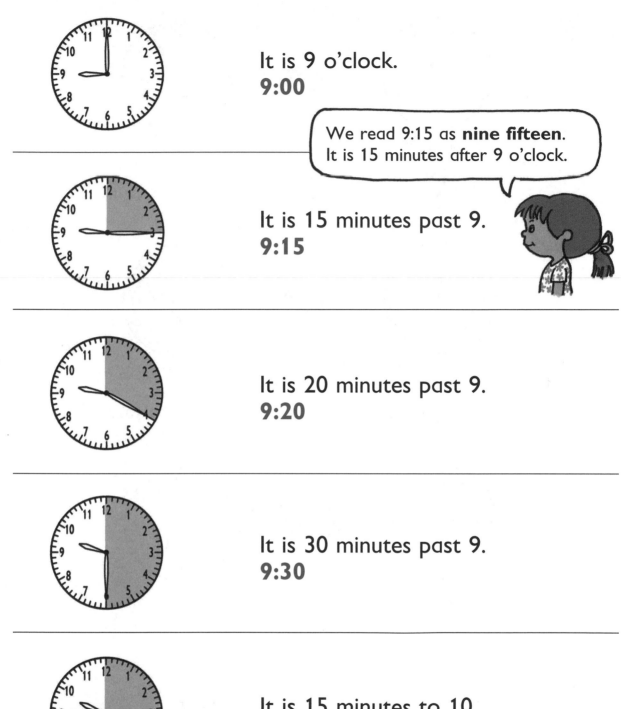

It is 9 o'clock.
9:00

We read 9:15 as **nine fifteen**.
It is 15 minutes after 9 o'clock.

It is 15 minutes past 9.
9:15

It is 20 minutes past 9.
9:20

It is 30 minutes past 9.
9:30

It is 15 minutes to 10.
9:45

9:45 is **45** minutes after 9 o'clock.
9:45 is **15** minutes before 10 o'clock.

1. (a)

1:00
1 o'clock

1:05
⬛ minutes past 1

(b)

2:00
2 o'clock

2:30
⬛ minutes past 2

(c)

4:45
⬛ minutes to 5

5:00
5 o'clock

(d)

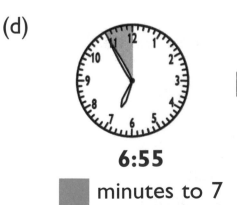

6:55
⬛ minutes to 7

7:00
7 o'clock

2. What time is it?

63

② Time Intervals

START

END

The television program starts at **9:10** a.m. and ends at **9.35** a.m. on Sunday.

It lasts ▢ minutes.

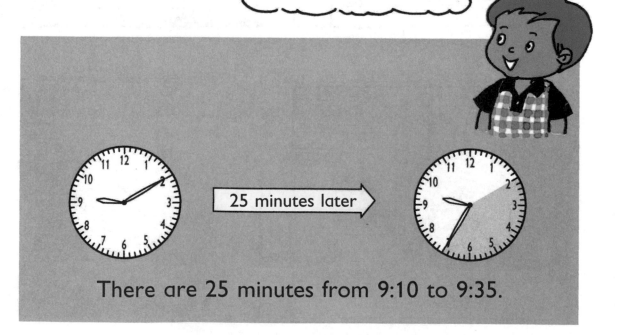

5, 10, 15, 20, 25 minutes

25 minutes later

There are 25 minutes from 9:10 to 9:35.

1. How long does each television program last?

		Start	**End**

(a)

Music time

(b)

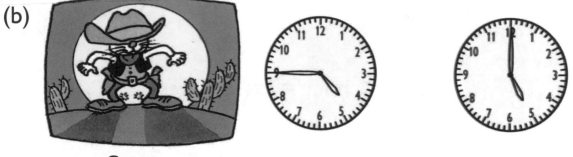

Cartoons

(c)

Story time

(d)

News

2.

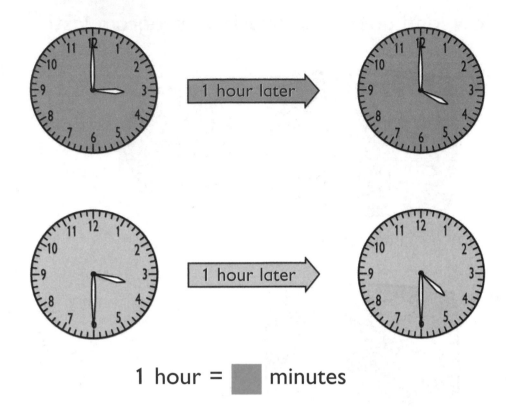

1 hour = ☐ minutes

3. (a) How many minutes are there from 3:30 to 3:55?

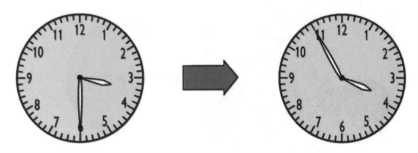

(b) How many hours are there from 5:45 to 11:45?

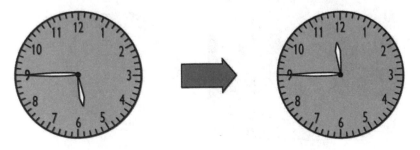

4. A test started at 10:40 a.m.
   It ended at 11:10 a.m.
   How long did it last?

   How many minutes are there from 10:40 a.m. to 11:10 a.m.?

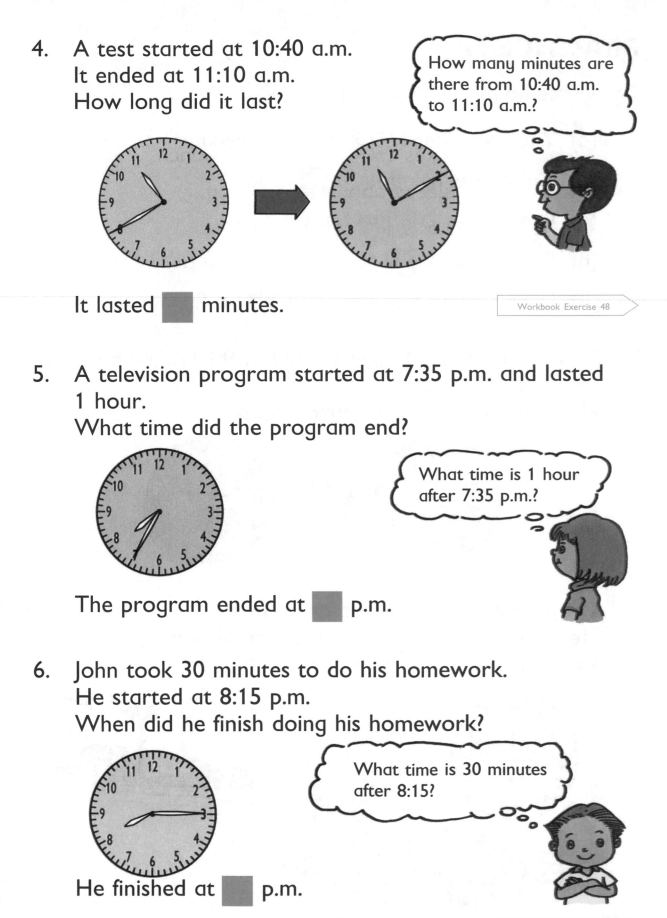

   It lasted ▢ minutes.

Workbook Exercise 48

5. A television program started at 7:35 p.m. and lasted 1 hour.
   What time did the program end?

   What time is 1 hour after 7:35 p.m.?

   The program ended at ▢ p.m.

6. John took 30 minutes to do his homework.
   He started at 8:15 p.m.
   When did he finish doing his homework?

   What time is 30 minutes after 8:15?

   He finished at ▢ p.m.

Workbook Exercise 49

PRACTICE 5A

1. Write hours or minutes in each ▉ .

    (a) Thomas takes 25 ▉ to have his lunch.

    (b) Carlos sleeps about 8 ▉ a day.

    (c) Rosa takes 2 ▉ to bake a cake.

    (d) Ryan takes 2 ▉ to swim 100 meters.

    (e) Lilian's shop is open for 12 ▉ on Sundays.

2. David's swimming lesson started at 9:10 a.m. and
    ended at 9:50 a.m.
    How long was the swimming lesson?

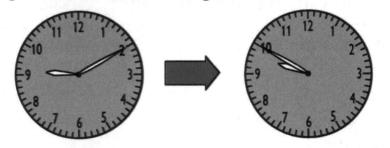

3. Mr. Johnson left his house at 9:45 a.m.
    He took 25 minutes to drive to the airport.
    What time did he arrive at the airport?

REVIEW D

Find the value of each of the following:

	(a)	(b)	(c)
1.	63 + 29	199 + 472	35 + 78 + 65
2.	554 − 183	463 − 398	500 − 75
3.	5 × 5	4 × 6	10 × 9
4.	18 ÷ 2	27 ÷ 3	50 ÷ 10
5.	$6.15 + $2.85	$7.05 − $5.55	$3.40 − $2.95

6. John had a rope 36 m long.
   He cut it into 4 equal pieces.
   Find the length of each piece.

7. 358 adults took part in a parade.
   169 of them were women.
   (a) How many men were there?
   (b) How many more men than women were there?

8. Amber bought 5 concert tickets at $7 each.
   How much did she pay?

9. John bought the can of milk powder and the jar
   of jam.
   (a) How much did he spend altogether?
   (b) He gave the cashier $10.
       How much change did he receive?

$1.80

$7.95

Capacity

1 Comparing Capacity

  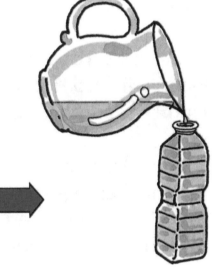

The jug holds more water than the bottle.

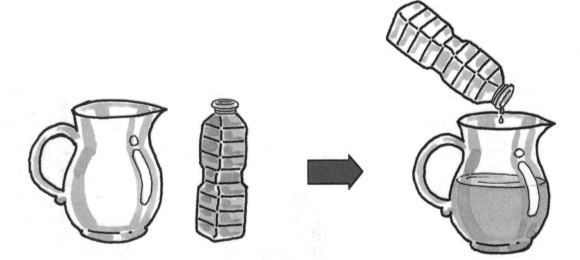

The bottle holds less water than the jug.

1. How many glasses of water does each container hold?

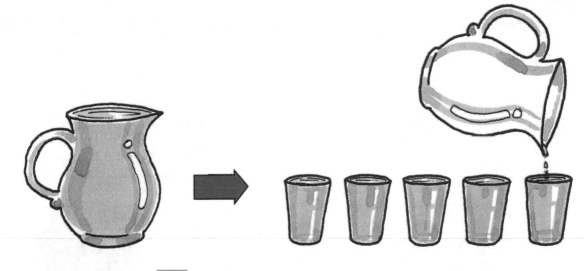

The jug holds ☐ glasses of water.

The bottle holds ☐ glasses of water.

2.

A   B   C

Which container holds the most water?
Which container holds the least water?

Workbook Exercises 50 & 51

Liters

Get a 1-liter beaker and find out how much 1 liter of water is.

We write ℓ for **liter**.

Get some paper cups.
Find out how many paper cups you can fill with 1 liter of water.

1.

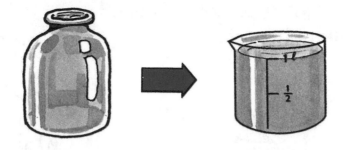

The bottle holds 1 liter of water.

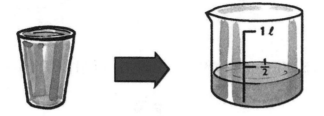

The glass holds less than 1 liter of water.

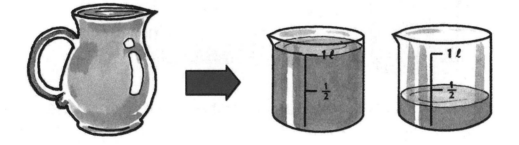

The jug holds more than 1 liter of water.

Which container holds the most water?
Which container holds the least water?

2. Mrs. Brown bought a carton of milk.
   How much milk did she buy?

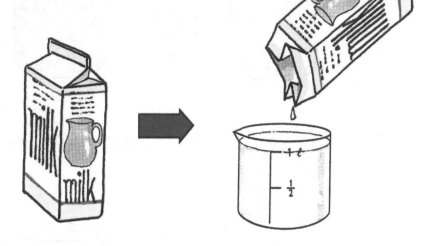

3. These two containers are filled with dishwasher detergent.

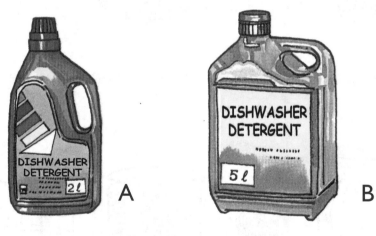

   A   B

   (a) Which container holds more dishwasher detergent?
   (b) How much more?

4. Get a bucket.
   Find out how many liters of
   water the bucket can hold.

5.

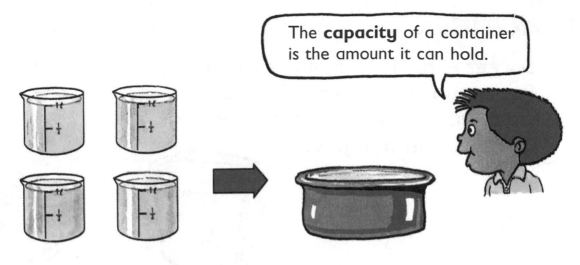

The **capacity** of a container is the amount it can hold.

The basin holds 4 liters of water.

The **capacity** of the basin is ▊ liters.

6. Make a 1-liter bottle.

Get a bottle which can hold 1 ℓ of water.
Pour 1 ℓ of water into it.
Mark the water level.

Use the 1-liter bottle you have made to find out the capacities of some containers.

Workbook Exercise 53

PRACTICE 6A

1. Bucket A holds 12 liters of water.
   Bucket B holds 8 liters of water.
   (a) Which bucket holds more water?
   (b) How much more?

2. Eric bought 20 liters of paint.
   After painting his house, he had 4 liters left.
   How much paint did he use?

3. A drinks-seller sold 52 liters of orange juice last week.
   He sold 38 liters of orange juice this week.
   How many liters of orange juice did he sell in the two weeks?

4. The table shows the amount of milk 3 children drink in a week.
   Find the total amount of milk they drink in a week.

Ben	6 liters
Emma	4 liters
Carlos	2 liters

5. A tank has a capacity of 30 liters.
   It contains 12 liters of water.
   How many more liters of water are needed to fill up the tank?

6. The capacity of a jug is 3 liters.
   Mrs. Beam needs 18 liters of fruit juice for her party.
   How many jugs of fruit juice does she have to make?

3 Gallons, Quarts, Pints and Cups

The capacity of a container can also be measured in cups, pints, quarts and gallons.

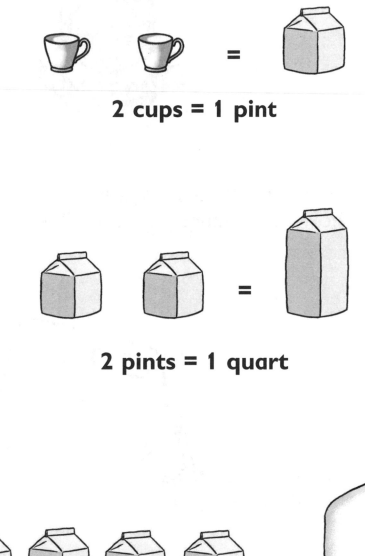

2 cups = 1 pint

2 pints = 1 quart

4 quarts = 1 gallon

1. Fill a 1-gal milk carton with water.
   Find out how many mugs you can fill with 1 gal of water.

2. These two containers are filled with milk.

Which container holds more milk?

3. Find a measuring cup with quart and pint markings.

   (a) Fill the measuring cup with 1 qt of water.
       Find out how many paper cups you can fill with
       1 qt of water.
   (b) Fill the measuring cup with 1 pt of water.
       Find out how many paper cups you can fill with
       1 pt of water.

   You can fill more paper cups with 1 ▮ of water.

4. Make a 1-pint bottle.

Get a bottle which can hold 1 pt of water.
Measure 1 pt of water in a measuring cup.
Pour the water into the bottle.
Mark the water level.

Use the 1-pint bottle you have made to do the following:

(a) Fill the bottle to the 1-pint marking.
Fill a cup from the bottle.
Can all the water be contained in the cup?

(b) Fill the bottle to the 1-pint marking again.
Fill a kettle from the bottle.
Can all the water be contained in the kettle?

5.　　**CUP　　PINT　　QUART　　GALLON**

Which of the above units of measure would you most likely use to measure:

(a) the amount of water in a fish tank?
(b) the amount of milk you drink daily?
(c) a carton of heavy whipping cream?
(d) a carton of fruit juice?

Comparing Quart with Liter

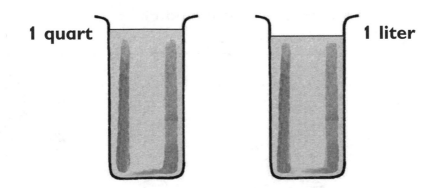

1 quart　　　　　　　　　　　　1 liter

1 quart of water is slightly more than 1 liter of water.

Workbook Exercise 54

REVIEW E

Find the value of each of the following:

	(a)	(b)	(c)
1.	327 + 498	135 + 465	209 + 591
2.	600 − 299	524 − 378	435 − 236
3.	8 × 4	5 × 6	10 × 8
4.	12 ÷ 2	30 ÷ 3	90 ÷ 10
5.	$3.75 + $2.55	$8 − $1.99	$6.20 − $4.35

6. 4 girls paid $28 for a present.
   They shared the cost equally.
   How much did each girl pay?

7. A magazine cost $5.80.
   A book cost $2.75 more than the magazine.
   Find the cost of the book.

8. Mr. Owens uses 5 liters of gas a day.
   How many liters of gas does he use in a week?

9. David took 35 minutes to cycle from
   his house to the library.
   He left his house at 10:45 a.m.
   What time did he reach the library?

10. 203 people took part in a singing contest.
    There were 128 adults.
    (a) How many children were there?
    (b) How many more adults than children were there?

Graphs

1 Picture Graphs

Count each type of fruit.

This picture graph shows the number of each type of fruit.

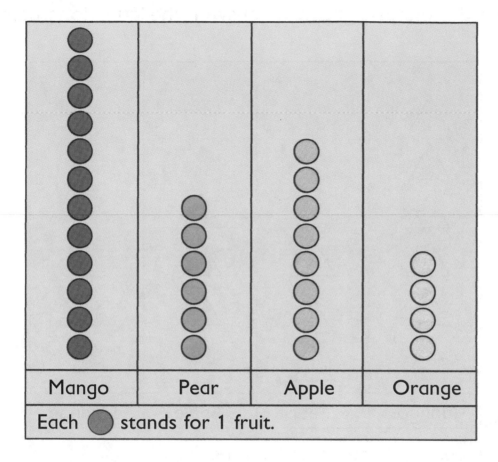

| Mango | Pear | Apple | Orange |

Each ⬤ stands for 1 fruit.

There are ▢ types of fruit.

There are ▢ mangoes.

There are ▢ pears.

There are ▢ apples.

There are ▢ oranges.

There are ▢ fruits altogether.

This picture graph also shows the number of each type of fruit.
Use the picture graph to answer the questions below.

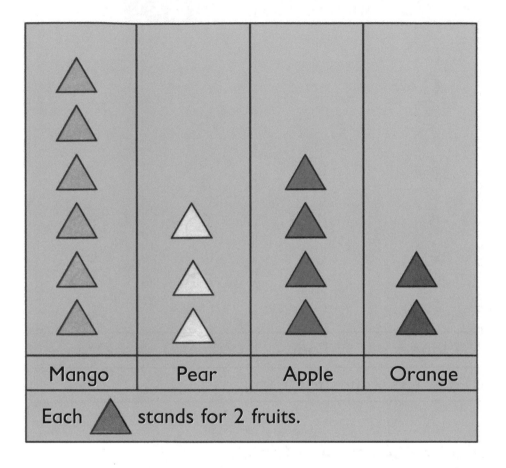

Each ▲ stands for 2 fruits.

(a) What does each ▲ stand for?

(b) What do ▲ ▲ ▲ ▲ ▲ ▲ stand for?

(c) How many more pears than oranges are there?

(d) How many more mangoes than apples are there?

(e) Which type of fruit is the greatest in number?

(f) Which type of fruit is the smallest in number?

1. A group of children made this picture graph to show the places they like to visit.

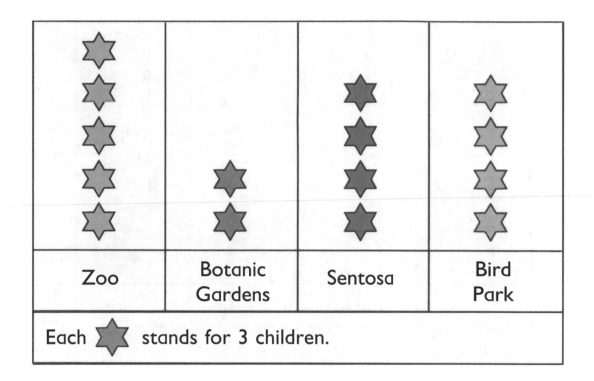

Use the graph to complete the following.

(a) ☐ children like to visit the zoo.

(b) ☐ children like to visit the Bird Park.

(c) 7 boys and ☐ girls like to visit Sentosa.

(d) The ☐ is the most popular place.

(e) ☐ more children like to visit the zoo than the Botanic Gardens.

Workbook Exercises 55 & 56

2. This picture graph shows the number of stickers four boys have.

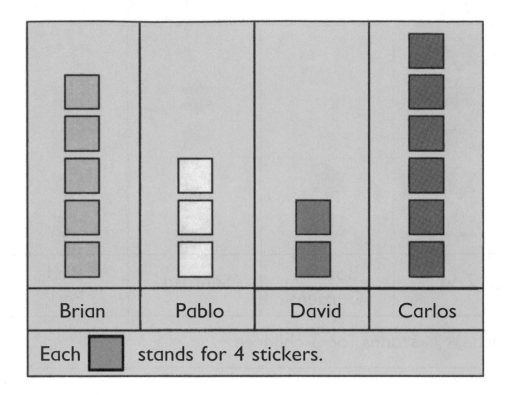

Brian	Pablo	David	Carlos

Each ☐ stands for 4 stickers.

Use the graph to complete the following.

(a) David has ▢ stickers.

(b) Carlos has ▢ stickers.

(c) ▢ has the most stickers.

(d) Brian has ▢ more stickers than David.

(e) If Carlos gives Pablo 4 stickers, Pablo will have ▢ stickers.

86

3. This picture graph shows the number of different types of fish sold by Justin.

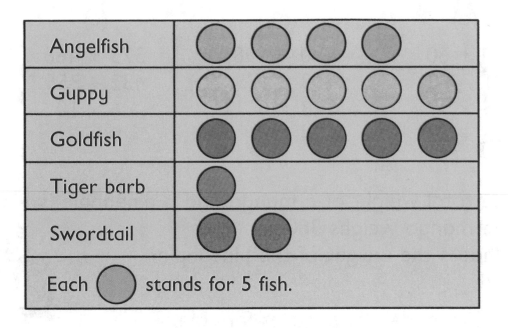

Angelfish	◯ ◯ ◯ ◯
Guppy	◯ ◯ ◯ ◯ ◯
Goldfish	◯ ◯ ◯ ◯ ◯
Tiger barb	◯
Swordtail	◯ ◯

Each ◯ stands for 5 fish.

Use the graph to complete the following.

(a) Justin sold ▢ angelfish.

(b) He sold ▢ more swordtails than tiger barbs.

(c) He sold as many ▢ as guppies.

(d) He sold ▢ goldfish and swordtails altogether.

(e) He sold all the goldfish for $2 each.
He received $ ▢ .

(f) He collected $30 for selling the swordtails.
He sold each swordtail for $ ▢ .

Workbook Exercise 58

REVIEW F

Find the value of each of the following:

	(a)	(b)	(c)
1.	749 + 60	590 + 198	375 + 466
2.	301 − 98	213 − 175	432 − 355
3.	5 × 2	3 × 8	6 × 10
4.	35 ÷ 5	24 ÷ 4	9 ÷ 3

5. The total weight of a mango and a pineapple is 950 g.
   The mango weighs 380 g.
   What is the weight of the pineapple?

6. Taylor made 300 pastries for sale.
   There were 12 pastries left after the sale.
   How many pastries did he sell?

7. Max packed 20 kg of rice equally into 2 bags.
   How many kilograms of rice were there in each bag?

8. Lindsey and her family drink 10 liters of milk a week.
   How many liters of milk do they drink in 5 weeks?

9. Mr. Ward sold 495 exercise books on Monday.
   He sold 98 fewer exercise books on Tuesday than
   on Monday.
   (a) How many exercise books did he sell on Tuesday?
   (b) How many exercise books did he sell on both days?

REVIEW G

Find the value of each of the following:

	(a)	(b)	(c)
1.	105 + 99	311 + 689	285 + 225
2.	527 − 418	306 − 98	700 − 652
3.	9 × 2	3 × 4	8 × 5
4.	16 ÷ 4	12 ÷ 3	70 ÷ 10

5. Jason cut 28 m of wire into pieces.
   Each piece was 4 m long.
   How many pieces of wire did he get?

6. A water tank can hold 250 liters of water.
   It has 185 liters of water in it now.
   How many more liters of water are needed to fill up
   the tank?

7. Mark bought 30 mangoes.
   He gave 14 of them to his friends.
   How many mangoes had he left?

8. Mary went to the library at 4:45 p.m.
   She left the library 35 minutes later.
   What time did she leave the library?

9. Tasha went to a bookshop with $9.
   After buying a book, she had $3.80 left.
   What was the cost of the book?

10. David eats 2 oranges a day.
    (a) How many oranges does he eat in 5 days?
    (b) How many oranges does he eat in a week?

Geometry

1 Flat and Curved Faces

Pair up objects of the same shape.

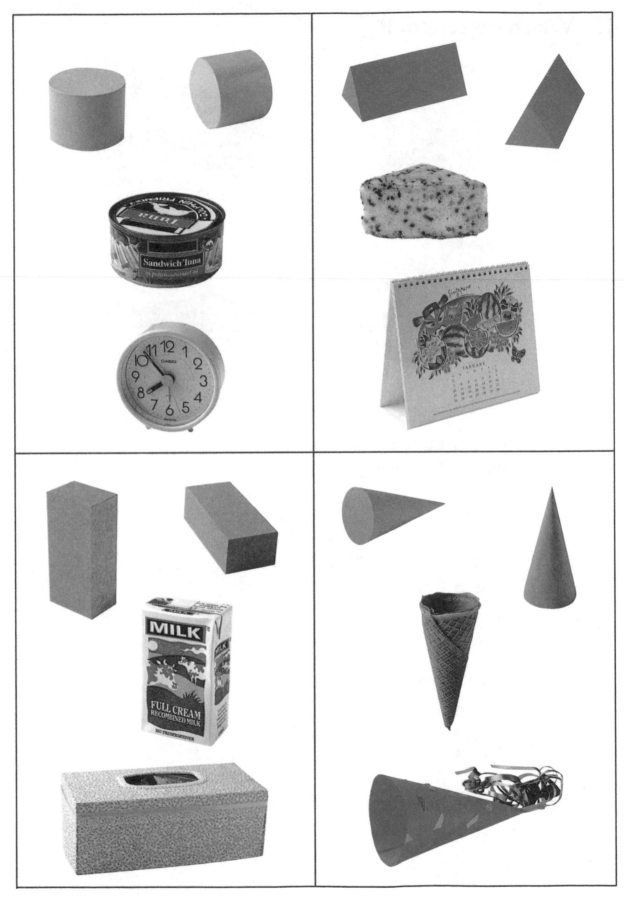

1. Which object am I?

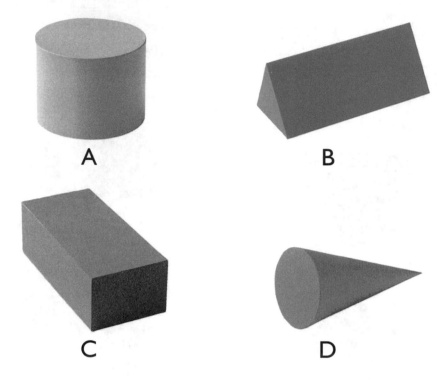

A

B

C

D

(a) I have a curved face.
I have 2 flat faces.

I am [ ] .

(b) I do not have curved faces.
I have **6** flat faces.

I am [ ] .

(c) I have a curved face.
I have only 1 flat face.

I am [ ] .

(d) I do not have curved faces.
I have **5** flat faces.

I am [ ] .

Workbook Exercises 59 & 60

2 Making Shapes

Kara fitted a square and two half squares together to make this shape.

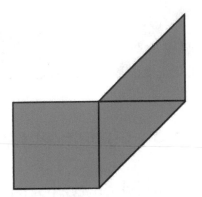

Melissa made a different shape.
She fitted a square and two half squares together like this:

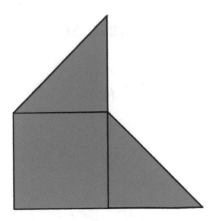

Use a square and two half squares to make another shape.
Compare it with your friends'.

1. These 4 triangles are of the same size.

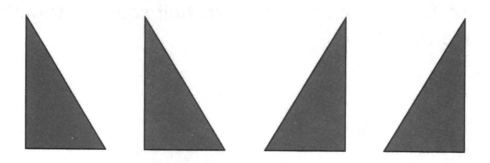

Trace the triangles on a piece of paper and cut them out.

Fit the 4 triangles together to form a shape like this:

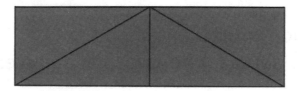

Find out how each of these shapes is formed by the 4 triangles.

(a) (b)

Use the 4 triangles to make another shape.
Compare it with your friends'.

2. (a) Draw and cut out a circle.
Fold it into halves and cut out the 2 half circles.

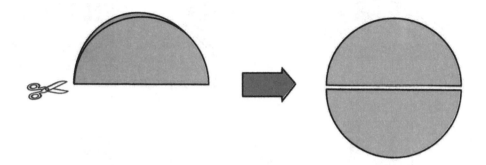

(b) Draw and cut out another circle of the same size. Fold it into quarters and cut out the 4 quarter circles.

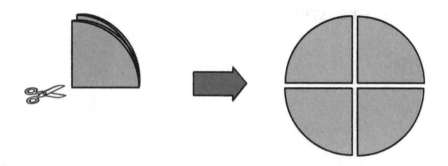

(c) Make this shape with a half circle and 2 quarter circles.

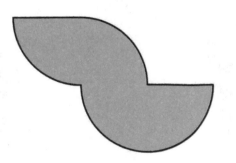

3. Use only two of these pieces to form a shape.

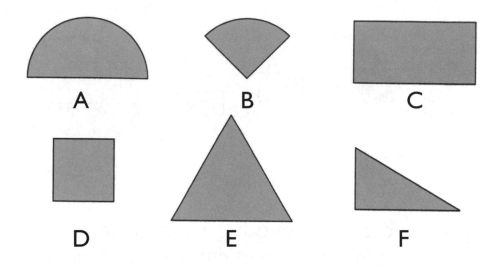

A B C

D E F

Here are some examples:

(a) (b)

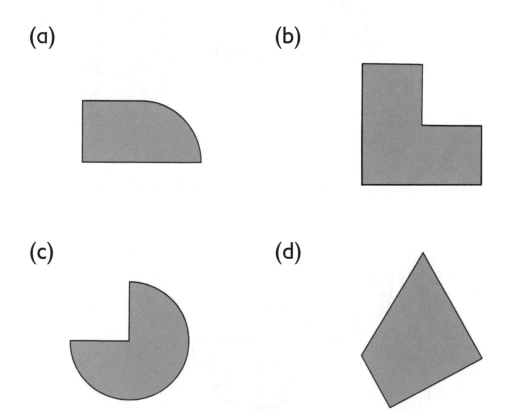

(c) (d)

Name the two pieces used for each shape.

Workbook Exercise 62

4. How many of these 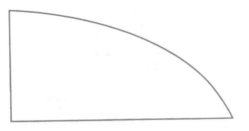 will cover the inside of each of the following figures?

(a)

(b)

5. This figure is formed by two straight lines and a curve.

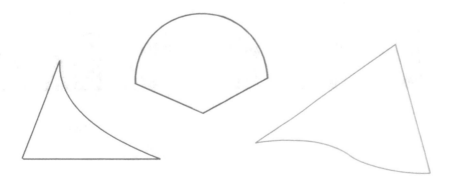

Here are some more figures formed by two straight lines and a curve.

Draw another figure with two straight lines and a curve.
Compare it with your friends'.

6. These are patterns of shapes.
What comes next in each pattern?

(a)

(b)

(c)

(d)

(e)

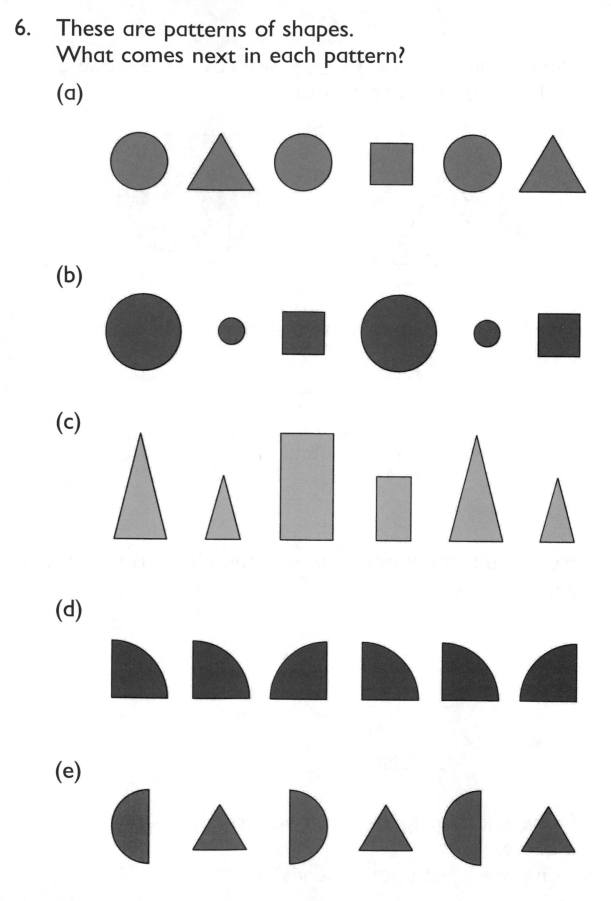

7. What comes next?

(a)

(b)

(c)

(d)

(e)

REVIEW H

Find the value of each of the following:

	(a)	(b)	(c)
1.	780 + 45	205 + 95	386 + 155
2.	425 − 265	632 − 473	500 − 197
3.	2 × 8	7 × 10	4 × 7
4.	32 ÷ 4	60 ÷ 10	50 ÷ 5
5.	$3.95 + $6.05	$5.08 − $3.99	$8.25 − $6.75

6. Find the missing number in each of the following:

(a) ▮ + 35 = 53   (b) 100 − ▮ = 85

(c) ▮ + 68 = 70   (d) 72 − ▮ = 41

(e) 28 + ▮ = 100   (f) ▮ − 46 = 37

7. What fraction of the shape is shaded?

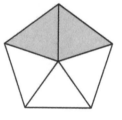

8.  stand for 32 oranges.

How many oranges does each ◯ stand for?

9. A concert started at 7:30 p.m.
It lasted 50 minutes.
What time did the concert end?

100

10. How many 50¢ coins can be changed for a $5 bill?

11. What is the weight of the box?

12. There were 275 passengers on a train.
    206 of them were adults.
    How many children were there?

13. Alice paid $6.50 for a skirt and $8.25 for a shirt.
    How much more did the shirt cost?

14. 1 kg of crabs costs $8.
    What is the cost of 5 kg of crabs?

15. Jeff bought a table and 3 chairs for $120.
    He paid $30 for the 3 chairs.
    (a) Find the cost of one chair.
    (b) Find the cost of the table.

16. 168 men, 287 women and 113 children took part in
    a parade.
    (a) How many adults took part in the parade?
    (b) How many more adults than children took part in
        the parade?

Area

1 Square Units

These shapes are made up of the same number of square tiles.

Each tile is 1 square unit.

The shapes are of the same size.
They have the same **area**.

The area of each shape is ◼ square units.

1. (a)

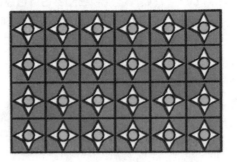

The area of the shape is [ ] square units.

(b)

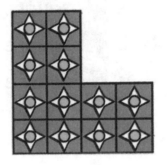

The area of the shape is [ ] square units.

(c)

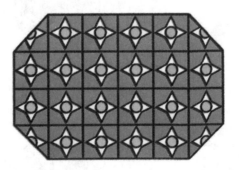

The area of the shape is [ ] square units.

2. Use square cards to make these shapes.

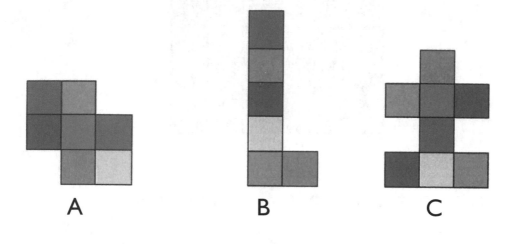

A   B   C

The area of Shape A is ▢ square units.
The area of Shape B is ▢ square units.
The area of Shape C is ▢ square units.
Which shape is the biggest?
Which shape is the smallest?

3. Which two shapes are of the same size?

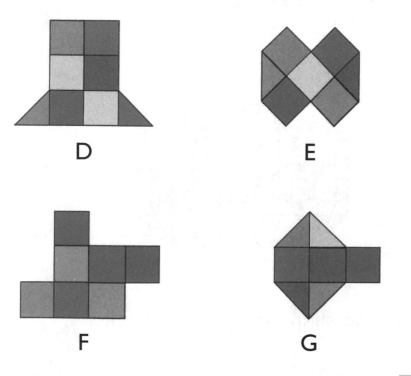

D   E

F   G

4. How many of these 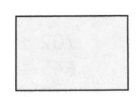 will cover the inside of each of the following figures?

(a)

(b)

5. What is the area of each of the following figures?

Each ▮ stands for 1 square unit.

P

Q

R

S

REVIEW I

Find the value of each of the following:

	(a)	(b)	(c)
1.	395 + 105	466 + 384	702 + 199
2.	555 − 75	800 − 197	645 − 386
3.	3 × 9	9 × 10	5 × 6
4.	14 ÷ 2	40 ÷ 4	10 ÷ 10
5.	$4.55 + $5.45	$6.95 + $2.25	$7.25 − $5.85

6. (a) What number is 10 more than 292?
   (b) What number is 10 less than 111?
   (c) What number is 100 more than 466?
   (d) What number is 100 less than 325?

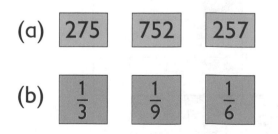

7. Find the missing number in each of the following:

   (a) 200 + ▨ = 270   (b) 632 + ▨ = 832

   (c) 452 − ▨ = 402   (d) ▨ − 9 = 900

8. Arrange the numbers in order.
   Begin with the smallest.

   (a) 275   752   257

   (b) $\frac{1}{3}$ $\frac{1}{9}$ $\frac{1}{6}$

9. Meiling has 4 fifty-cent coins and 3 five-cent coins. What is the total amount of money in dollars and cents?

10. David is running in a 100-meter race.
    He is **48 m** from the starting point.
    How many meters is he from the finishing point?

11. A supermarket opens from 11:00 a.m. to 9:00 p.m.
    every day.
    How many hours a day is the supermarket open?

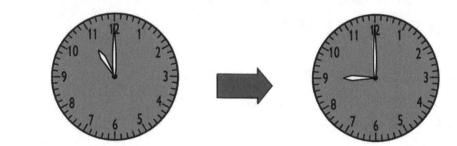

12.

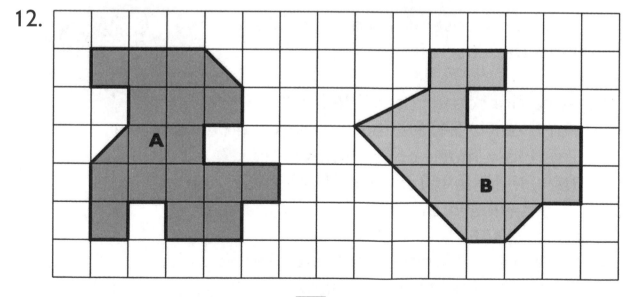

The area of Shape A is ⬛ square units.

The area of Shape B is ⬛ square units.

Which shape is bigger, A or B?

13. Lindsey takes 2 hours to sew a dress.
    How long does she take to sew 5 dresses?

14. Mrs. Wells bought some cans of sardines for $16.
    Each can of sardines cost $2.
    How many cans of sardines did she buy?

15. Carla wants to buy a doll which costs $8.60.
    She has only $6.80.
    How much more money does she need?

16. There were 305 boys in a school hall.
    There were 46 fewer girls than boys.
    How many girls were there?

17. Peter used 128 liters of gas last month.
    He used 25 liters more gas this month.
    How much gas did he use this month?

18. The total cost of 4 plates is $24.
    Find the cost of one plate.

19. A refrigerator costs $960.
    An oven is $425 cheaper than the refrigerator.
    (a) How much does the oven cost?
    (b) Find the total cost of the oven and the
        refrigerator.

20. Ryan read 10 pages of a storybook a day.
    After reading the storybook for 6 days, he still had
    24 pages to read.
    (a) How many pages did he read in 6 days?
    (b) How many pages were there in the storybook?

REVIEW J

1. The total length of 2 pieces of ribbon is 9 in.
   One piece of ribbon is 5 in. long.
   Find the length of the other piece of ribbon.

2. 1 lb of grapes costs $3.
   Mrs. King bought 7 lb of grapes.
   How much did she pay?

3. Nicole used 24 yd of cloth to make dresses.
   She used 4 yd of cloth for each dress.
   How many dresses did she make?

4.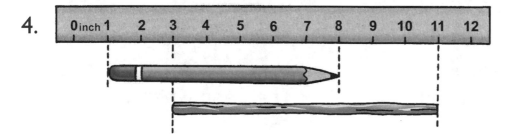

   Which is shorter, the stick or the pencil?
   How much shorter?

5. A store sold 302 qt of milk last month.
   It sold 29 qt more milk this month.
   How much milk did the store sell this month?

6. A tank can hold 115 gal of water.
   It contains 38 gal of water.
   How many more gallons of water can be poured into
   this tank?

7. John weighs 65 lb.
   His sister weighs 19 lb less.
   What is the weight of his sister?

8. Ryan had a rope 18 yd long.
   He cut it into 3 equal pieces.
   Find the length of each piece.

9. 1 ft = ⬛ in.

10. There are ⬛ cups in a quart.

11.

The watermelon
weighs ⬛ lb.

The pear weighs
⬛ oz.

12. Jason drinks 2 c of milk daily.
    (a) How many cups of milk does he drink in 6 days?
    (b) How many cups of milk does he drink in a week?

13. Eric paid $45 for 5 lb of shrimps.
    What was the cost of 1 lb of shrimps?

14. 1 yd of cloth costs $3.
    Kathy bought 9 yd of cloth.
    How much did she pay for the cloth?

15. An apple and a peach weigh 15 oz.
    The apple weighs 8 oz.
    What is the weight of the peach?

110

16. How many quarts of water can be poured into a 1-gal container?

17. Emily needs to tie 4 presents of the same size with ribbons.
    She uses 2 yd of ribbon for one present.
    How much ribbon will she need to tie all the presents?

18. A bag of carrots weighs 14 oz.
    A bag of lettuce weighs 3 oz less than the bag of carrots.
    (a) What is the weight of the bag of lettuce?
    (b) What is the total weight of the two bags?

19. Sara cut 16 ft of string into 4 equal pieces.
    What is the length of each piece of string?

20. One bag of sugar weighs 2 lb.
    How much do 10 bags of sugar weigh?

21. Use your ruler to draw a line 9 in. long.

22. Emma weighs 59 lb.
    Her mother is 78 lb heavier than she.
    (a) Find the weight of Emma's mother.
    (b) What is the total weight of Emma and her mother?

23. 28 qt of water is poured equally into 4 containers.
    How much water is in each container?

24. A piece of ribbon is 1 m long.
    A piece of string is 1 yd long.
    Is the ribbon longer than the string?

25. Scott uses 2 c of milk to make one pudding.
He wants to make 7 puddings.
How many cups of milk does he need?

26. What is the total length around the triangle?

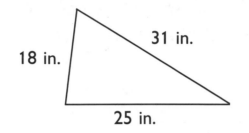

27. Ryan walked 470 yd to a gift shop. He then walked another 250 yd to the post office.
How far did he walk?

28. David weighs 65 lb. John weighs 127 lb. Amy weighs 88 lb.
(a) What is the total weight of David, John and Amy?
(b) How much lighter is David than John?

29.

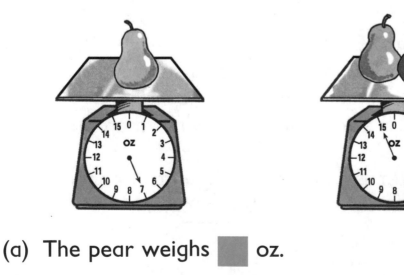

(a) The pear weighs ⬜ oz.

(b) The apple weighs ⬜ oz.

(c) Which weighs more? How much more?